MALCOLM MOOI

INDIGO CHILD
CHASING DREAMS MONEY CAN'T BUY

Indigo Child
Chasing Dreams Money Can't Buy
First Edition, First Impression 2017
ISBN 978-0-620-76817-7
Copyright © Malcolm Mooi

Published by:
Inspired Publishing
PO Box 82058 | Southdale | 2135
Johannesburg , South Africa
Email: info@inspiredpublishing.co.za
www.inspiredpublishing.co.za

© All rights are reserved. Apart from any fair dealing for the purpose of research, criticism or review as permitted under the Copyright Act, no part of this publication may be reproduced, stored in a retrieval system or transmitted, in any form or by any means, electronic, mechanical, photocopying, recording, or otherwise, without the prior written permission of the copyright holder.

Table of Contents

Dedication		9
Introduction – A Hero's Journey, a tribute to Joseph Campbell		10

PART 1 – NOTHING IS EVER QUITE WHAT IT SEEMS

Chapter 1	Origins	19
Chapter 2	The Wonder Years	31
Chapter 3	Anfield Dreaming	37
Chapter 4	Lucky Number Seven	49
Chapter 5	How Deep Does the Rabbit Hole Go?	75
Chapter 6	Rehab	79
Chapter 7	There are Far Worse Things than Death	87
Chapter 8	That One Time I Stopped Time	93
Chapter 9	Living on the Edge of Chaos	101
Chapter 10	Why can we Remember the Past, but not the Future?	125
Chapter 11	She gave me a Watch, when all I Wanted was some of her Time	141
Chapter 12	I'll be Happy When...	153

PART 2 – INTO THE DEPTHS OF DARKNESS

Chapter 13	The Coloured Delusion	159
Chapter 14	The Story behind the Story	165
Chapter 15	Intellectual En-Slave-ment	171
Chapter 16	Failure to Launch	177
Chapter 17	The Enablers	181

PART 3 – ATONEMENT

Chapter 18	The Story behind the Story behind the Story	191
Chapter 19	Celebrating Life and Diversity	197
Chapter 20	Different Perspectives	201
Chapter 21	Finding Purpose through Entrepreneurship	207

Dedication

To my parents Allen and Adele, for your unconditional love and unwavering support.

Introduction:
A Hero's Journey, a tribute to Joseph Campbell

Joseph Campbell (March 26, 1904 – October 30, 1987) was a world-renowned mythologist, writer and lecturer, who was best known for his work in comparative mythology and comparative religion, covering many aspects of the human experience. His philosophy is often and simply summarised by "Follow your bliss". His work has had a profound effect on my life, which is not surprising as he has had a major influence on generations of creative artists. His work was used by Abstract Expressionists in the 1950s and is still being used today by contemporary film-makers as a means to express drama, storytelling, myth, religious ritual and psychological development. George Lucas was an avid admirer of Campbell's writings and used them as a direct reference in his creation of Star Wars. Other blockbuster movies which used this structure include The Matrix, Superman, Lord of the Rings, Spider-Man, the Wizard of Oz and the Lion King.

In his book, The Hero with a Thousand Faces, Campbell explores the theory that important myths from around the world which have survived for thousands of years all share a fundamental structure that is common to all heroic tales in every culture. This common structure forms part of a universal pattern that is popularly known as a Hero's Journey.

The hero is a personification of a culture's mythology, someone who has given his or her life to something bigger than themselves. Traditionally, the hero may have been a warrior, the ideal of strength and courage; an explorer, the founder of civilisations; a philosopher, an adventurer of the mind. In a modern world, artists, activists, scientists and entrepreneurs add to the pantheon of heroes.

Sadly, we are living in a period of mythological decay – mythologies that once built civilisations are no longer relevant to a world which is now one global interlocked community that is driven by information. As a result, we are seeing individuals living in response to outside factors like information and commands, a society that has people pulling back into their own groups – black power, white supremacy and privilege, capitalists, religious and political factions and extremism, patriotism, blue collar workers, white collar workers etc. to support mythological systems that are outdated and divisive. We are left to ask ourselves: what group do we identify with or belong to, instead of following what comes from within? What enlivens our hearts and wakes us, what new wisdom and treasures are we bringing back to transform our world for the better?

Regardless of one's own context, the Hero's Journey is essentially the same – one shape-shifting story of the vision quest that transforms the world. Whether it was Odysseus, Jesus, Muhammad, Buddha, Luke Skywalker, Neo, Frodo, or Nelson Mandela – the hero is the one who responds to their call to adventure.

The story often opens with the hero appearing restless, uneasy or unaware; something is missing in life, there is a feeling of destiny, but the hero as yet does not know what that is. The hero feels the fear of the unknown and tries to turn away from the adventure, reluctant, however briefly. Others may express the uncertainty and danger ahead to support the hero's reluctance to accept their call to adventure. It is a time for separation, and sometimes it takes a shock or traumatic experience to make the final break from the past in order to gain the necessary courage to accept the call. A defining life-altering moment.

Once the call is accepted, the hero reaches within to a source of courage and wisdom. Nobody can go at it alone however, and every hero needs a mentor or support system to provide them with wisdom, training, equipment or advice that will help them on their journey. The descent into the underworld of adventure is often blocked by strange and dangerous threshold guardians; they mark the point of no return. Beyond them is the region of the unknown, a dreamlike labyrinth of tests and trials with unfamiliar rules and values. It is a time to sort out allegiances and newfound allies to prepare for the major challenges in the unknown world. To pass this initiation, the hero must become a dragon slayer who seizes the moment to retrieve the treasure or rescue the princess. But the decisive ordeal of the quest is when the hero confronts death or faces their greatest fear. The hero is challenged to the point of following the wisdom of his or her heart, allowing for death and rebirth. Out of this moment of death comes a new life.

Joseph Campbell was fond of recalling how Schopenhauer, in his essay 'On the Apparent Intention in the Fate of the Individual', wrote of the curious feeling we can have of there being an author somewhere writing the novel of our lives, and in such a way that through events which seem to us to be chance happenings there is actually a plot unfolding of which we have no knowledge. To quote Campbell, "When you follow your bliss, the universe will open doors where once there were only walls". There is something about the integrity of life when following your heart; the universe moves in and helps you.

The hero takes possession of the treasure won by facing death. There may be celebration, but there is also danger of losing the treasure again. The hero is driven to complete the adventure, leaving the unknown world to bring the treasure back home. At the climax, the hero is again severely tested on the threshold of returning home. He or she is purified by a last sacrifice, another moment of death and rebirth, but on a higher and more complete level. By the hero's action, the polarities that were in conflict at the beginning of their call to adventure are finally resolved. The hero returns home or continues the journey, bearing some element of the treasure that has the power to transform the world, just as the hero has been similarly transformed.

Joseph Campbell believed that the seat of the soul is there where the inner and outer worlds meet. The outer world is what life throws at us, while the inner world is our response to it, and it is where these two come together that myths are created. The outer world changes with historical time; the inner world is the world of the human spirit which is constant throughout mythological systems and time. We will always have a sense of recognising something, and what we are recognising is our own inward life inflecting through history. The search for purpose and meaning is one of the most powerful and lasting themes in every culture since the dawn of time. The function of the hero is making the inner world meet the outer.

Indigo Child

Indigo Child is a journal of sorts, documenting the key moments in my life, including accepting my call to adventure and reflections from the unknown and unfamiliar as my hero's journey unfolds.

PART 1

NOTHING IS EVER QUITE WHAT IT SEEMS

CHAPTER 1
ORIGINS

Chapter 1
ORIGINS

I fell into this realm on January 29th, 1979 at 9:55 am, born at the Florence Nightingale Hospital in Hillbrow to Allen and Adele Mooi, a forceps birth indicative of my reluctant, stubborn and rebellious nature something I brought with me as opposed to personality traits developed. If you didn't know, a forceps is a surgical instrument resembling a pair of tongs used by doctors for grabbing and manoeuvring a baby's head to help guide an infant struggling to leave the birth canal. Physically, it left me with an oblong-shaped head. Emotionally, it exposed my susceptibility to attachment. Symbolically, it has set the tone for much of how my life has unfolded.

My infant and toddler years were full of joy and love. I had both my parents, both sets of grandparents, a brother Jonathan who arrived within two years and a huge extended family of aunts, uncles and cousins. Our generation comprised a mischievous group of boys who wreaked havoc and terror when the family got together. My mother's parents formed the nucleus of our family, Clifford and Yvonne Smith, or as we affectionately knew them, Ouma and Oupa. A doctor by profession, my grandfather gave me a sense of invincibility. When we fell ill, he saw to us and in no time we'd be back to mischief and terror. My father's parents, John and Leah Mooi, or as we fondly knew them, Grandma and Oupa Johnny were just as present during these early stages. Grandma looked after us when mother dearest returned to work. From what I can recall, Oupa Johnny said little, mostly sitting on the stoep smoking his pipe, alternating between reading the newspaper and staring out the window observing the goings-on in the park. His arms were marked with tattoos, an anchor and a dragon covered his forearm. When Grandma struggled to contain our naughtiness, he stepped in, flexed his bicep, twisting his wrist outwards as a warning that the dragon was angry and likely to spew fire. Ever inquisitive, I noticed my grandfather scratching on his tattoos. On the rare occasion he entertained a conversation, I asked him why, and learnt what the word 'regret' meant; the conversation ever so brief as he shifted his attention back to his pipe and reading the newspaper. Grandma was much more active and managed the household – cooking, cleaning and minding the kids. She too gave me a sense of invincibility. While frantically working through her daily cleaning routines, she'd strap me to a harness hung from the kitchen doorframe. Seeking attention, I'd move in her direction, the cables keeping me suspended momentary in the air – I thought I could fly! It was the first time I experienced frustration. Firstly, by not having the ability to fly at will or understanding the relationship of the cable and harness to my perceived ability, and secondly, then having difficulty explaining it to adults.

I attended preschool opposite the park from my grandparents' house in Coronationville, and recall little from this time apart from developing an interest in art, Michael Jackson's hit music video 'Bad', which felt like a feature movie, and the ever-present smell of smoke emanating from the chimneys in the late afternoon. It was how I knew it was time to be fetched by the parentals. Drawing consumed my time, and when I couldn't perfect drawing, I traced pictures in a quest for symmetry and the right ratios – an early sign of my creativity, attention to detail and Obsessive Compulsive Disorder (OCD) tendencies. It was a time of immense joy when Oupa bought a holiday home in Ifafa Beach, an hour south of Durban. I experienced beach sand under my feet, the taste of salt water and dizziness when getting knocked over by a wave. The world was bigger than just visiting my grandparents or walking across the park to attend preschool. Endless fun, not a worry in the world. This would soon change.

Entering grade school represented a curtain being unveiled to show a harsher reality.

I was raised a Christian and attended the local Anglican Church. As far as formalities went, the kids attended Sunday school and then joined the main service to see the adults take communion. I enjoyed Sunday school, the stories and lessons gave me a sense belonging outside my immediate family. The ideology was easy to understand: anything good, we gave praise to God; anything bad, we blamed the Devil. Disobey and God would punish you to hell. Guilt was something I became familiar with very early in life. I still have a vivid memory of attending church which differed from other occasions, when I experienced the presence of God for the first time. It was the usual transition from Sunday school into church for the closing processions; the adults went up for communion with us kids filling the front pews as the congregation sang to their hearts' content. I looked around, observing the pianist at the organ, the adults queuing up to take communion while others knelt down with their hands extended as the priest handed them bread wafers and wine, which we were told represented the body and blood of Christ who had died for all our sins. A wave of emotion washed over me. I felt immense warmth, joy and love. I told my mom and it pleased her; it was a proud and dear moment.

Once released from church, we returned to our mischievous ways, playing games with toy guns and terrorising the girl cousins. We even formed a gang and assumed roles based on characters from the popular TV series, the A Team. I chose Mad Murdoch – yes, in part because of my identification with his eccentricities and fuzzy logic, but more so with my reluctance to lead our four-man gang. As a kid, I couldn't wait to grow up, always questioning my parents about how much longer it would be before I could take part in communion or start 'big school'. And when big school arrived, it wasn't worth the wait. In class, we were placed in groups based on reading ability. I was in the slow readers' group and despite extra effort, remained there. With my performance in class not improving, my mother took me to see a psychologist, Anna Venter. It was the first white woman I interacted with. After a few assessments, Anna Venter diagnosed me with daydreaming, and reported that I didn't want the responsibility of being the older brother subject to harsher rules and discipline. She also noted the close relationship with my cousins as a cause for concern. Born in January, the education system dictated I start school a year ahead of my cousins. It turns out I was doing poorly in class with aspirations of failing so I could join them the following year.

I attended T.C. Esterhuysen Primary School for Grade 1 to Grade 6, a public school in Riverlea, a 'coloured' township within the city of Johannesburg. Apartheid and segregation were unknown to us until a bunch of friends were bullied by white kids. Race became ever-present in our conversations and centred on people we had never even met – white people, black people, where we fit in, naïve regurgitated opinions taken from our homes – whites were superior, blacks were inferior, and we were in the middle. These opinions formed our core beliefs that defined our self-worth and what we were capable of. It influenced the way we dressed, spoke and even the music we listened to. We dressed to imitate gangsters making us look tougher than we were. Our ambitions included flicking a Buck folding pocketknife to expose the blade and popping a beer, getting the cap off by using another bottle. We spoke slang that accentuated our accents with greetings like "Awe masekind" or "Fede hond", translating to "Hi, how are you" and "What's happening in your life, dawg"; and when somebody spoke clearly, we'd call them out for "twanging", inferring they're trying to be white. Music confused me most, with 'coloured' music being based on genres and not actual coloured musicians. Being famous or accomplished seemed to be reserved for the other races. The race agenda was ever-present in these formative years.

My family is a spectrum of shades, ranging from ghostly white to chocolate brown skin. Our family therefore wasn't immune to apartheid's divide and conquer strategy, with preference going to the fairer-skinned family members with straight hair and light eyes, while the darker-skinned ones with curly hair faced ridicule, being called a "kroes kop" or told "don't behave like a darkie". I developed my first insecurity. Ashamed of failing the pencil test, I nagged my older cousins about when I'd grow my Chinese hair. But more about this later…

Primary school was memorable. Our teacher was off sick one day so we spent the day in another classroom. The class was writing a test so the teacher kept yelling for us to keep quiet. Defiant and persistent in our tomfoolery, I laughed so much that I farted! I was sharing a chair with a friend, the base of which was plastic, so the fart went off like a machine gun – dhak! dhak! dhak! dhak! dhuck! dhuck! dhuck! dhadak! dhadak! – everything happening in slow motion, the class all lifting their heads in sync to see what the commotion was. I jumped off the chair, pointed and shouted, "Sies, you farted!" to my friend, who stared back in disbelief. The other memory involved a crow chasing me on the school playground. This bird was possessed by a demon, forcing me to hide in the toilets to escape its torment. Such was the trauma that birds still scare me, even today. The other significant memory was an excursion to Gold Reef City, an amusement park built on an old gold mine which closed in 1971. It was a fun-filled day and our class got to go down a mine shaft that was 57 levels (3,500 metres) deep. Afterwards, we took a group photo as a souvenir. In the picture, I noticed myself somewhat distanced from my classmates. It was a realisation of being different, a feeling that has been persistent throughout my life.

I saw less of my father's parents once I started primary school, our visits limited to occasional Sunday lunches. Oupa Johnny developed gangrene from diabetes and had his right leg amputated, severely limiting his mobility in the final years of his life. I recall visiting him in the hospital the night before his passing. He was unconscious and breathing via a ventilator, his lungs moving to the haunting sound of water bubbles motioning in his chest. When we received news of his passing, my parents broke down in tears. I stood by wondering why they were crying and why tears had not reached my eyes. At his funeral, Grandma walked up and placed her hand on his coffin, bidding him farewell until they'd meet again. It was a touching moment that influenced my desire to one day grow old with a soul mate. My father had me when he was 35 years old. There is an 8-year gap between him and my mom. We have been at loggerheads for as long as I can remember, my dad always one step ahead in curbing my tomfoolery. He had two personalities: one was strict and serious, a disciplinarian; the other, a joyous drunk. During the week, I wished for the joyous drunk so the rules weren't enforced, and we didn't have to watch the 8 o'clock news or get scolded for the day's shenanigans. Weekends, I longed for a strict and serious dad, one who didn't embarrass us with his drinking, progressing from silliness to a slurred voice to red spots on his neck and face, which culminated in him passing out on the couch. Our relationship wasn't always tense. As a baby, my father would put me to sleep, holding me in his arms as we listened to music. I would raise my hand and rub his ear to form my first habit. It gave me a sense of comfort. When I was younger, I would play with the ears of anybody willing, provided they were cold. Warm ears were of no use to me and numbed the sensation between my fingers. During adolescence, when childhood habits became embarrassing, I would play with my mother's ears in the privacy of our home to avoid ridicule, and in adulthood, this habit continued in relationships with significant others.

Christmas was a special time of the year; it was the birth of Jesus and family holidays spent at the coast with all the cousins. I'm not sure how everybody fitted into that two-bedroom house with one toilet, but we managed with much ease. How cool was it getting presents on Jesus' birthday! One year, we received watches as gifts. During the night of Christmas Eve, my uncle had too much to drink and went to sleep on the veranda for fresh air. Burglars gained entry into the house and robbed us, our watches were amongst the items stolen. The following year, we received remote-controlled cars for Christmas. My parents convinced us to leave the cars at home based on what had happened the previous year. It made sense, only to then come home from holiday to find our house burgled and the cars gone. Another year with no presents! More than that, intruders had got into our home and violated our place of safety, leaving us afraid to sleep at home for weeks to come. I'll admit, it still scares me as an adult to sleep in a house alone.

We were active growing up and took part in several sports. Saturday mornings we played soccer at the grounds in Bosmont, our parents standing along the touchline as we ran around like dancing ballerinas. We gathered at my uncle's house afterwards to watch games from the English Premiership League, our family split between Liverpool FC and Manchester United. We were die-hard Liverpool fans. Golf was another sport we played and enjoyed, but never excelled in. My parents also had us play the piano. It was a talent hidden from everybody and only exposed at school when our English/Music teacher ordered me to recite a poem as punishment for being disruptive. My reading ability was poor, so I requested to play the piano instead. The class gasped in disbelief as I played Beethoven's 'Fur Elise'. It was the first time I distinguished myself from the 'slow readers' club. On another occasion, we learnt about abbreviations and had to give the full word from abbreviated words written up on the blackboard. Most of the abbreviations cleared apart from one, G.P.O. The class was stumped, and even the smart kids couldn't solve it. I stared at the letters G. P. O., raised my hand and answered General Post Office. I expected to be wrong, a sentiment supported by groaning classmates, "No, that can't be it", only for our teacher to confirm "That's correct Malcolm".

My preteens were an age of rebellion and enlightenment. I recall trips to Soweto to visit our grandparent's domestic worker. Gerty had helped my grandmother with cleaning duties and raising the kids for many years, so much so that she was considered family. Soweto was vibrant and fun, we played in the streets and observed the hustle and bustle of township life. Those visits stopped when it became dangerous and I sensed the seriousness of apartheid. It also led to a defining moment, my parents removed us from the public schooling system and placed us in Sacred Heart College, a private school in Observatory.

Private school was a rude awakening. I had to repeat Grade 6 as they felt I wouldn't cope with Grade 7. Most revealing though were all the ill-informed views I had about other races. I met white kids who didn't hate me and became good friends. I met black kids who were smart and spoke better English than me and even met kids from other countries. We were all just friends. It was hard to process how one school had more facilities than our entire suburb. It was a whole new world and I fell in love with it. It introduced me to Hip-Hop music, which was much more appealing than 'coloured music'. The more I immersed myself in this new environment a mere 25-minute drive from home, but worlds apart from our isolated coloured community, the more I broke set beliefs. So began a habit of questioning everything and trusting nothing.

The first was our financial status. Until that point, I believed us to be wealthy. We were never lacking, vacationed at our family's holiday home on the coast and attended private school. One afternoon our clique met outside our house and money was up for discussion. Boys being boys, we each took turns to boast about how much our dads earned and how much money they had in their bank accounts. We were millionaires. Later that evening, I asked my dad about our financial affairs. He appeared uncomfortable, but entertained me nevertheless. It turns out we weren't millionaires, didn't even have R100,000 in the bank, nor R10,000, nor even R1,000. We were just about making ends meet. I regretted asking after sensing that my father felt somewhat defeated by my disappointment. The same disappointment turned into embarrassment when my dad started dropping us off and picking us up from school in his faded yellow 1975 Toyota Corolla. My brother wasn't shy to ask him to pick us up a block away from the school to avoid the other kids from finding out.

The second was religion. What we learnt in Sunday school and church resembled nothing that I had been observing in life. It was the complete opposite – family feuds, cheating husbands, gossip, dishonesty, racism, one priest carrying a firearm and another comforting women in the congregation. The list goes on, and things that were once distant stories which only happened to other people, got closer to home. I became less and less interested in attending Sunday school or church, and it became a battle on Sunday mornings as I pleaded and reasoned with my parents not to go, even questioning why my father didn't attend church, only for him to remind me about his younger days as an altar boy to justify why he no longer had to go. They stood firm, though I was disillusioned and started to bunk church, roaming the streets instead. My dad caught us and threatened to destroy my music collection, my most prized possession: TDK cassettes housed in a customised shoebox, decorated by famous brands and provocative rebellious words sourced from newspaper and magazine clippings. I snuck the box out of the house to a friend's place for safekeeping, and agreed to attend church until my confirmation. But it was too late. I attended church, but lost my belief in God and identified as an atheist. One word can sum up my teenage years: awkward. By age 13, I was wearing size 8 shoes, with long, narrow feet and skinny legs. Mood swings, the-world-owes-me attitude and general aloofness earned me the nickname 'Go Slow'. A visit to the optometrist confirmed I was near-sighted and had to wear spectacles. My vanity couldn't handle being called 'four-eyes', and so began years of misunderstanding – not seeing what was on the blackboard in class so it affected my grades, responding to people when I wasn't being spoken to, and labelled a 'high bug' for not greeting. The whole high bug label bothered me, not so much that the only reason I didn't greet back was because I couldn't see, but four years into a private school education meant a widening gap of indifference. I never thought I was better than anybody else, but the mindset and conversations were different, the exposure was different, the aspirations were different. Sacred Heart College attracted students whose parents were leading the liberation struggle, the likes of Ramaphosa, Slovo and most notably, the Mandelas. I actually had the privilege of seeing Nelson Mandela. He attended our school's swimming gala, sitting at the opposite end of the pool. As the races finished, he'd acknowledge us kids with a gentle nod and smile as we passed by him. To be honest, I didn't understand who he was or that he would become our first democratically elected president, but he stood out and had stature, humility and grace about him. I played soccer at school and was selected to be captain, only to pass the accolade on to somebody else, so avoiding having to read out our team's result at the school assembly. I also played soccer for our neighbourhood team, which was different. At school I was talented, at home I was lucky to be a squad player; such was the pool of talent from our community. One guy was likened to Brazil's Roberto Carlos and took part in the World Cup in France in their youth curtain-raiser games, and he was so talented he received an invitation to trail at Barcelona FC, which he never pursued. It baffled me: such an opportunity was so far out of reach for us, why wouldn't anybody take it? While friendships at school thrived, they all but deteriorated in our community. It turned into an unhealthy rivalry of us versus them, bickering and fights which escalated to a guy getting shot and killed less than a kilometre from our house.

It was a turning point; our innocence lost. What if we had been in the park that night? I distanced myself from people in our community.

The moment had come for my confirmation at church, but instead of receiving the Blood and Body of Christ, I received my Church Leaving Certificate. The symbolism long lost as I expressed views to the dismay of my mother, "Do you know who else eats bodies and drinks blood? Cannibals and vampires."

CHAPTER 2
THE WONDER YEARS

Chapter 2
THE WONDER YEARS

In my haste to grow up, high school arrived, and with it, romance. A first kiss and a relationship that spanned high school and first year university. An on-again off-again romance which so followed the plot of the award-winning TV series, The Wonder Years, my tough love family even referred to us as Kevin and Winnie. In the final episode of The Wonder Years, there is a voice-over with children heard in the background, "Growing up happens in a heartbeat. One day you're in diapers, the next day you're gone. But the memories of childhood stay with you for the long haul. I remember a place, a town, a house, like a lot of houses. A yard like a lot of other yards. On a street like a lot of other streets. And the thing is, after all these years, I still look back... with wonder."

And so, I wondered about our fate and whether it would end as did Kevin and Winnie's? We'd make it work I reasoned, I'd make sure of it. As we entered high school, brand name clothing became a top priority. No longer could you wear clothes from retailers like Ackermans or Pep Stores; it was now Cutty Sark jeans, a Polo t-shirt and All-Star sneakers. After school we'd hang out at her house, but I had to be gone before her father got home from work. We'd chat, listen to music, do homework, make snacks. Time with her was different compared to hanging out with boys and the usual tomfoolery. In one of our afternoon chats, she expressed disappointment at her father's refusal to buy her a pair of All Stars. This became my mission. I negotiated with my father to wash his car every Saturday for two months to raise the money needed to buy her a pair, keeping it a surprise for her birthday. Now, anybody who knows me will appreciate the magnitude of this gesture, as I avoided household chores like the plaque. And so our relationship followed a pattern of on-again (me pursuing) off-again (her breaking up) romance. It was anything but physical. I cherished our friendship so much that I didn't attempt anything beyond first base at the risk of losing her.

Chapter 2: The Wonder Years

1994 was a defining moment for our country as we transitioned to a democracy. It was defining for me too as I completed Grade 9 and was progressing to senior High School. My parents sat me down and told me they could no longer afford the fees at Sacred Heart College and were enrolling me at Roosevelt Park High School, a "model C" public school.

The news was devastating. I might as well have died, and so I did.

For the next three years I vowed not to make any friends at the new school or take part in anything, sports included. The first few months were the worst. I became so despondent my teacher eventually called my mother in to alert her I was suffering from depression. We fought daily and I ran away from home. Let me elaborate... I was giving my mother the toughest of times and my father was running out of patience. I was used to getting hidings throughout my life, and my father even had a whip he called "the riempie" as a last resort to instil discipline. He had a system where he'd count until three before unleashing it on us: "One... Two..." and we'd fall in order. As we grew older, we became more defiant. When my dad started his count "One... Two..." we'd finish it for him – "Three!" and take the hiding. This day was different though. We had just sat down for dinner, an argument ensued and my mother broke down, "Don't you care that you may lose your family?", to which I replied, "It's no loss...", to which my father unbuckled his belt. The first blow hit my head, the belt wrapping around my forehead. I didn't even lift my hands to shield the blows. Food flew across the living room and decorated the floor as my father unleashed whip after whip. I just sat there, numb, defiant. I didn't get up for school the following morning; instead I packed a bag, decided I was dropping out of school and leaving home. No sign of where I was going, I just left. My mother got home from work and my brother broke the news. I can't even imagine what horrible thoughts might have gone through her mind, but I had just gone up the road to my uncle's house. My parents had no clue where I had gone, and my mom thought I was wandering the streets of Hillbrow, the notorious inner city neighbourhood considered to be the most dangerous in Johannesburg. It was only when my cousin Mark called them much later that they came to know of my whereabouts.

I expected another beating from my father, but he remained calm. After a lengthy discussion, they convinced me to return home. As I entered the house, I could hear my mother still crying in her bedroom. I went back to school as promised, but remained despondent and disengaged for the remaining three years. It was the last hiding I ever received.

Quiet and distant, my classmates tried and failed to get me to make peace with my situation. One guy stood out in particular. He carried a Bible with him everywhere. Day after day he persisted, always proposing that I read the Bible to find peace. I read the verse he mentioned to get him off my back. When we met the next day, I told him it made little sense – which it didn't. He then shared his story. He wasn't always the goodie-goodie we knew; he had a troubled past and it was only when he gave his life to God and the church that his life changed for the better and he became a model student. I attempted to deter him by questioning if God even existed, which only motivated him even more. I always found it amusing to see believers and the conviction in which they defended God. All his efforts weren't enough to convince me. I can't recall any of the scriptures he quoted, but one thing he said has stuck with me. Once he gave himself to the Lord, he stopped getting sick and when he felt a cold coming on, he prayed and the symptoms ceased.

While friends back at Sacred Heart College were making the most of senior high, I was 16 years old and stuck in a deep and dark rut refusing to leave like I did my mother's womb. My only joy: a part-time job secured at Edgars, a clothing retailer, as a cashier. I was independent and had the means to buy name brand clothing. I also started a habit of saving money. My dream was to travel the world.

1995 saw the launch of Windows 95, redefining home computing and my life. In our family, my mother's eldest brother Winston was always the first to do things – first to drive a fancy car, start a business, travel to America, and own a home computer and a cell phone. We spent hours at their place, glued to the screen taking turns to use Microsoft Paint and a choice of games. We surrounded the PC awaiting our turn to play Fifa 95, with Liverpool FC versus Manchester United the preferred teams. Our inquisitive nature also meant we explored system folders, clicking on and deleting files to see what would happen. Blue Screen! "System Failure: An error has occurred." Reboot, same message. Panic set in; this would be the death of us. We spent hours trying to bring it back up, even reading the manual with no luck. We had to fix it and fast before my uncle found out! All we had were the 13 floppy disks which contained the installation files, so we attempted to reinstall the Operating System. Everything we knew about computers was self-taught, and through a process of trial and error, we formatted the hard drive before reinstalling the OS. It was working again! Hotmail launched in 1996 and then Napster in 1999. The world was changing! Why send or receive mail via the post office when I had email? Why buy music when I could download it off the internet, for free!?

School was still a drag and it showed in my results. My teacher resolved that I switch to standard grade Maths, which I refused, instead opting for extra Maths lessons, attending Master Maths every Wednesday afternoon for the next two years. If I ever stood a chance of going to University, I needed to pass higher grade Maths for an exemption.

I matriculated in 1997 and was free from 'prison' for a crime I didn't commit. I applied to study at Wits University. The motive: reunite with some of my Sacred Heart College classmates. My results weren't good enough to do a B Comm Degree so I settled for a BA General taking Sociology, International Relations and Statistics. The plan: get into a B Comm. The motive: resume The Wonder Years high school romance as Winnie also took Sociology and International Relations. However, within the first month I became disillusioned, bunking class to sit and socialise on the grass or shoot pool. By the end of the year I had failed Statistics 101, and the only marks I got were for writing my name on the answer booklet. I passed the other subjects though, where it wasn't so much about facts as long as you could back your stance. I informed my parents of the decision not to go back to university, seeking employment instead. My parents, ever concerned as to my short-sightedness arranged for me to meet a career guidance counsellor. How could I throw away the opportunity to study at university, an opportunity they were robbed of under apartheid? As fate would have it, a close friend had just finished school and enrolled at Wits Technikon to do a National Diploma in Computer Systems Engineering. When I saw the curriculum, I knew it was for me, thinking back to the time we restored the Windows Operating System. With registrations closed, I faced the prospect of having to wait a whole semester before applying, so on opening day I stood in line for five hours to speak to the Dean of Engineering about late applications. From the shouting heard down the corridor, Mr Fouche would take much convincing to accept my late application, but he did! I could be charming when the need arose. Technikon was different. It was 50% theory and 50% practical lab work. I attended all my classes and enjoyed learning for the first time. There were still serious gaps in my learning abilities, again reflected in my results, but something changed – my attitude. Over the next four years I progressed from just scraping through, to average, to passing Mathematics with a B average, to achieving distinctions in both my majors. Was I capable? I was more than capable. But, as reluctant as I was to leave my mother's womb, I delayed my practicals to only graduate three years later in 2005. In the time that had passed, Wits Technikon merged with other tertiary institutions to form what is now the University of Johannesburg.

Grandma died in 2000 after a long bout with illness. In the days leading up to her death she mentioned that our late grandfather had come to fetch her. When asked what she told him, she replied, "I told him to wait, I'll come when I'm ready!" She was such a feisty larger-than-life woman who filled our lives with joy.

In the final episode of The Wonder Years, Winnie leaves to study Art History in Paris while Kevin stays in the United States. They write each other once a week for eight years. When Winnie returns to the United States in 1982, Kevin meets her at the airport with his wife and eight-month-old son. In my real-life version, it was a case of 'Winnie' sending a mutual friend to speak about us dating again. This time she was sure she was ready. It was an opportunity I couldn't decline after months of not talking. There was a different feel to our relationship, a sureness that it could last more than a matter of months.

And so we resumed spending time together, this time alternating between our homes. While things changed, some things stayed the same. I could spend as much time as long as I wasn't there when her father returned home. On

Chapter 2: The Wonder Years

one occasion, we were in her bedroom and I was sitting on her bed while she blow-dried her hair, when there was a knock at the door. We weren't expecting anyone, so she went to check. I remained in the bedroom to see her father walking down the passage towards me. I sat frozen on the bed, unable to move, scared for my life. But somehow he didn't see me? He turned right into his bedroom to put his coat down. Winnie followed and asked me, "Did he see you?" No, I nodded, still frozen to the bed. She grabbed my hand to escape, my left foot latching onto a bag that lay on the floor. We made a dash for it, dragging the bag all the way down the passage. How he didn't hear the commotion remains a mystery. My intentions were pure and I couldn't understand what this man had against me, but it didn't matter. Frustration mounted as Winnie became annoying; she knew exactly which buttons to push to get under my skin, eventually prompting me to break up. It was only after a week that the true nature of her sudden ability to annoy me surfaced: she had met somebody, an older guy. The same mutual friend sent to get us back together this time delivered news of her newfound love, including a very detailed description of how she had lost her virginity. The news made me nauseous and sent me into a rage. I vowed never to speak to her again, ever. I also 'shot' the messenger. It marked the end of childhood friendships.

CHAPTER 3

ANFIELD DREAMING

Chapter 3
ANFIELD DREAMING

And so I entered adulthood. Mission: Lose my virginity. We were out one night at a club and this girl kept smiling at me. I smiled back but didn't have the courage to speak to her. At the end of the night, she walked over to us, handed me a piece of paper and said, "Here's my number, call me". My parents were away for the week and I was home alone. Perfect opportunity! I'll call her, invite her to the movies and dinner, and then back to our house. I rehearsed my lines a dozen times and called. "Hi, it's me... would you be…" I'm not sure how much I said, but she stopped me and said, "Look, I go for lunch soon, pick me up from work and we have an hour". "What will we do in an hour?" I enquired, to which she replied, "Have sex hun". Losing my virginity was like a scene out of the hit movie comedy American Pie. My thrusting rhythm was like a broken staccato melody and if there were candles lit, the house would have burnt to the ground. Before processions were over, she let out what sounded like a proper fart. It was traumatising. Later I learnt it was a 'fanny fart'. And so began a decade of adventure-filled conquests!

It was around this time that Lucas came into our lives, an exchange student from Switzerland who was living in Soweto before it became a popular tourist destination. He was facing a difficult time as his host parents were never home. When my mom heard his story, she offered to have him live at our house for the rest of his stay. Lucas stood out like a sore thumb living in Soweto, and this was the case in Riverlea too, being the only 'white' person among coloureds. But this didn't faze Lucas. He was just relieved not to come home to an empty house and even used public transport to get to school. I recall the awkwardness of having to show him where the taxi rank was as the thought of having a white person live with us hit home; "I knew he was a high bug" hidden in the stares of people we passed on the street, "He thinks he is better than us, he thinks he's white". Observation: Swiss white was different to South African white. As the weeks passed, so did the misconceptions. Lucas wasn't burdened by the race filter, bringing me to the realisation that it made no sense to hold onto mine. It was a welcomed relief. Lucas could play the piano by ear, so the hopes of my father investing in a piano all those years earlier were justified as Lucas entertained us with his amazing ability. His stay with us was memorable and, before returning home to Switzerland, Lucas made one more visit to Soweto – to braid his hair. Strange, coloured people were trying everything to straighten their hair, and here was this white person going for an Afrocentric look. The bond forged saw him return frequently, even bringing his girlfriend to meet us. He was our other brother.

In my final year of studies, I taught Computer Literacy at Future Kids. I felt so intimidated and out of my depth, especially with the four-year-olds. It was amazing to see how fast the kids learnt compared to adults. It came as a surprise when the owner one day told me that of all the instructors, the kids said I was their favourite.

After five years of saving, I had accumulated enough money to travel abroad, breaking tradition to host a big party as was the case with 21st birthdays, when a hall was decorated and filled with family and friends – the parties were legendary. Instead, I elected to travel with Mark to London for three weeks. The plan, a road trip to Anfield, home of Liverpool FC, the football club I had idolised since childhood. It was the first time I kept a journal, detailing the experience in a scrap book; an outlet for the creative energy I had been suppressing.

16 June 2000, Friday

Flew to London via Frankfurt (Germany) on SAA flight 206. Take off was incredible! Nothing but little kraals throughout Africa. Flying above the clouds was amazing, like a blanket covering the sky, and the stars could not be clearer. Mark got drunk but denied it. Lots of turbulence (cool). Airplane food sucks! Storm!!! Cool!!! Flying above the lightning gives you a whole new perspective. Yeah – went upfront to the cockpit!!! There are so many buttons and stuff. Best view in the world! I realised how drunk I was... had to focus not to fall over. Chatted to this dude who I thought was the co-pilot, asking him lots of questions about planes and flying. This fool played along.... Turned out he was just another passenger. Go Slow! No more drinking!"

17 June 2000, Saturday
"Dusk... a rainbow through the clouds (breath-taking). Mark still drunk from night before, remembers nothing. Flew over Italy (just saw lights). Altitude: 29,000 feet; Speed: 907 km/hour. Flew over the Swiss Alps (there is a God!). Landed in Frankfurt 6:15 am (8 °C) — liars. Mark got us lost, but I was there to lead the way. Flew to London (Heathrow) on Lufthansa flight 4544. I'll never get enough of a plane taking off. Mark hijacked the window seat :(Flying is boring. Annemie picked us up at the airport using a taxi that caters for VIPs, SLK 500 baby! Took a 1,5 hr boat ride up the River Thames. The English drink beer, SPIT! Had to force myself to drink it. Geez, I'm drunk again.... This trip is nothing what I expected it to be. The buildings and architecture are so old yet the vibe in the city is amazing! So many cultures in one place! Saw the Houses of Parliament; Big Ben; Westminster Abbey; Buckingham Palace.... Used the tube and caught a taxi home. A real eye-opener, their transport system is so efficient. Got to meet the Queen (joking). Just a picture from Madame Tussauds."

18 June 2000, Sunday
"Went to a BBQ at Debbie's... interesting afternoon, very interesting!!! Talk to my agent ;) 10 pm and the sun is only setting."

Present Day: "Talk to my agent" exposed me to the world of cougars. This lady believed I was a professional soccer player and wanted to represent my interests!

19 June 2000, Monday
"Went to Kingston, walked through Bentall Centre. Had lunch at Frere Jacques (French). Had a few beers... Appreciating beer! Cooked supper that night — chicken and pasta. Went to the Thames to watch the sunset. Time: 9 pm. What a view, plus seeing all the planes coming into Heathrow. A plane lands about every two minutes. Had a few more beers, went home and tanned my ass."

20 June 2000, Tuesday

"Went to Bath (the city), one of the oldest in the UK. Saw the Roman Baths; Pump Room Bath and Bath Abbey. Watched
England exit Euro 2000 against Romania. They used to bury the dead 'inside' the church."

21 June 2000, Wednesday

"Bettie's (I mean Elizabeth's) birthday. Drove to the countryside, to an exclusive club. Five beers cost us 21; a three-night stay is 2600 — WOW! Exchange rate = R10,38." :)

22 June 2000, Thursday

"Spent the day on the underground. Took +/- 20 trains. Went to Piccadilly Circus, Harrods, Leicester Square, SOHO and the London Eye."

23 June 2000, Friday

"Took a drive to the countryside. Went to a toga party in Kensington. The apartment was on the 4th floor and the balcony looked onto Princess Di's palace. Met people from all over the world, either working or studying in the UK. Something to think about doing. Adele will miss me though! Watched the sun set at 10 pm... saw it come up at 4 am (weird). I witnessed this couple doing the deed in the lounge, they thought I was sleeping — so erotic. Made my way home at 10 am — first time I used the tube by myself — yay!"

24 June 2000, Saturday

"Recovered for most of the day. Went to Uncle Lionel and Aunty Liz for supper. It was an entertaining evening; he reminds me so much of my grandfather, his gestures and use of entertaining anecdotes when telling a story."

Present day: Uncle Lionel was an anti-apartheid activist and the youngest of the 155 accused along with Nelson Mandela in the 1956 Treason Trial. After being acquitted, he resumed careers in journalism and political activism. In 1960, he spent five months in prison during the state of emergency declared after the Sharpeville massacre. Following his release and the likelihood of being rearrested, he fled the country and lived in Ghana, then China, before settling in Britain. He went on to become the first black President of the National Union of Journalists, trade unionist, author and chairman of the Notting Hill Housing Trust, which saw him earn an OBE for his work in this field.

25 June 2000, Sunday
'Chilled at the river.'

26 June 2000, Monday
'Spent the day walking through Leicester Square... Went on this wicked virtual roller-coaster ride. The chick operating the ride was cute. Sexy accent... We exchanged numbers.'

27 June 2000, Tuesday
'Went to Camden Town but the flea market is only open on weekends.'

28 June 2000, Wednesday
'Took a ferry from Westminster down to Tower's Bridge. Had supper at a pub just off the river.'

29 June 2000, Thursday
'Spent the day walking through Richmond town.'

Chapter 3: Anfield Dreaming

1 July 2000, Friday
"Went to the German School Festival (Debbie's kids go there), then down to the river, then to the movies... 6 to see Three to Tango — say what!? Plus the screens are soooo small." :)

2 July 2000, Saturday
"Went to Camden Town. Walked through the flea market. Had my palms read (freaky). Then to Hyde Park (Speaker's Corner). It is massive!"

Present Day: The palm reader told me I would travel the world and only find my soul mate to settle down with late in life.

3 July 2000, Monday
"Hired a Mercedes A Class and took a road trip exploring the UK... if only we could find our way out of London. It's such a mission. First stop — Stonehenge. It was unbelievable being there! Decided to do a tour of the south west. Drove until 1 am in the morning. We couldn't find accommodation so we slept in the car in the middle of nowhere (scary). Stonehenge — forever a mystery.

4 July 2000, Tuesday
"Made our way to Tintagel Castle, the legendary birthplace of King Arthur. Showered at a caravan park. What an amazing place; landed up spending most of the day checking the sites. Not wanting to sleep in the car again we went in search of a youth hostel. I was driving and kept missing the turnoffs, landing up in Manchester. Went to Old Trafford — what is all the fuss about? When we were in the parking lot, a few limos pulled up and dropped people off. We thought it was players but it turned out to be a school banquet. It was getting late, and we still didn't have accommodation. Annemie was in Warrington on business so we drove up and spent the night in her room."

5 July 2000, Wednesday

"If I died today, my life would be complete — went to Liverpool, Anfield Stadium Driving up to the stadium is amazing, unbelievable, larger than life, outta this world!!! :) Took the tour of the stadium (money well spent). Had to beg Mark to come along (he's a Manchester United supporter, but I needed somebody to take the pictures); the bastard even made me pay for him. First, they take you through the players' entrance, then you go to the change rooms. The whole tour is designed to make you experience a typical match day at Anfield. Visitors' change room first. Mark took a piss in the toilet. Next up is the home team change room (can life get any better?). When you walk in, the players' T-shirts hang like they would on match day, starting with the goalkeeper... defenders... midfielders... strikers.... The tour guide then told us that those were actual T-shirts worn by the players (LFC T-shirt vs jail as I weighed up stealing Robbie Fowler's #9 jersey...). Then you make your way through the tunnel onto the field, touching the LFC 'This is Anfield' plaque that so many greats have touched. :) As you walk onto the field they play a match day sound clip of the crowd cheering, a life-changing experience! Seeing the stands, the pitch... something that will stay with me forever!"

6 July 2000, Thursday

"Went to London Dungeon. Some crazy messed up stuff happened in the old days... the way they tortured people — OUCH! Then off to the Tower of London. Saw the crown jewels, explored different sections of the castle. Heard some brutal stories of how people got beheaded — 1,500 bodies are buried under the church floor... We met Aunty Liz and walked along the river. Passed Shakespeare's Theatre. Went into the Design Museum and then to the Tate Art Museum/Gallery."

Chapter 3: Anfield Dreaming

7 July 2000, Friday

"Today we went to Wembley Stadium. It's tiny compared to TV, even the twin towers. Then we walked down Oxford Street, went into Hamleys, Levi's, Virgin, Disney... Walked to Piccadilly, saw people parachuting, a live band on the back of a truck. There is so much to see and do! Saw weird people today — a whale of a woman spoke to herself and was very fidgety. A man on the tube was knitting and there was a group of seriously drunk people."

9 July 2000, Saturday

"Flying home today :(Having such fun, plus today is the Concert in the Park. We locked our luggage at the station and went to the concert. When we got there Destiny's Child was performing. It was crazy! Haven't seen so many people in one place! Geez, we're gonna miss our flight! We caught the express train direct to Heathrow and had to run through the airport to check in on time... London-Frankfurt-Home. What an experience!"

I returned home restless and frustrated. My only comfort was creating a collage from all the pictures taken to match my journal entries. It took five years to save enough money for the trip to London. The mission: make enough money to travel every three years.

I secured a job as a PC technician serving small-and medium-sized businesses. It was the owner, PA and two technicians. A job that lasted only nine months. The experience was great, the compensation model questionable. I couldn't accept the amount of revenue generated off my time and effort versus what I was getting paid. It was skewed in favour of the owner and escalated to my first standoff with the upper echelons of management. We presented our case to the owner for his consideration. He tested our resolve knowing I had just bought my first car by rejecting our proposition. So, just as the other technician took up an offer at one of our clients leaving me solo, opportunity presented itself: I was in a car accident. The car was a write-off and the insurance settled the outstanding balance, so I resigned. My next move: work for a corporate, something more structured where I could build a career. I committed to this being the only choice.

CHAPTER 4

Lucky Number Seven

Chapter 4
LUCKY NUMBER SEVEN

High Performance Systems (HPS) ran an intern programme which I applied for, only to end up waiting ten months for a reply that never came. Had it not been for a family connection being the HR director at HPS, I would not have gotten an interview. Even then, preparation is everything. Before securing an interview, I studied their company website, their history, products and leadership. The story of their founders was so inspiring. Their lives and achievements, extraordinary – and it all started in a garage! The CEO at the time was a female CEO; how progressive I thought in this male-dominated industry. The interview was conducted by two hiring managers. Like the time I had to convince Mr Fouche to accept my late application to Technikon, or for Winnie to be my girlfriend, I was my charming self. They sat at the opposite end of the table taking notes as I replied to their questions. I secured the internship! Sometime later, my manager told me how they fought over who I'd be assigned to.

In the ten months prior to this I was at home with not much to do, waiting in limbo to secure a job at a corporate, so my father proposed reading a book. I didn't give it much thought – reading was his thing, not mine. He nevertheless persisted, and I reluctantly accepted the book he handed me, Kane and Abel by Jeffrey Archer. It remained on my bed pedestal for weeks more. To read a 557-page book was insurmountable. Reading had never interested me. It had haunted me throughout school, from the 'slow reader' group days at TC Esterhuysen Primary School, to experiences at Sacred Heart College and then Roosevelt Park High School. In Grade 7, our classroom was arranged in groups of six, two people to a desk. For reading, we went around the class, each person given a paragraph. I was so ashamed that I counted ahead the number of paragraphs until my turn and rehearsed to minimise my exposure, often missing the lesson's aim. Then in Grade 8, we had an English project that involved us creating our own story books. In one activity, they paired

Chapter 4: Lucky Number Seven

us with learners from Grade 2, where we had to read to them and find out what they liked to help us with ideas for the mini books we'd be writing. We worked in groups of four, two Grade 2s and two Grade 8s taking turns to read. When I heard how well the Grade 2s could read, I realised just how bad I was and turned on the charm to keep them reading. Relief! My struggle was again exposed in the final year of school when I had to read the part of 'Malcolm' in the set piece Macbeth by William Shakespeare.

And so at 23 years of age, I read my first book: Kane and Abel. It set my life on a new path. Those opening few chapters were hard to get through, using parts of my brain that were easily rendered by TV. I had to build all the characters, what they looked like, how they dressed, what they sounded like, the locations and the ambience they had described in the book, all while keeping the plot fluid. My imagination switched on and I was hooked after a few days, reading into the early hours. I developed an unquenchable thirst that has seen me read every day ever since.

We were 24 interns on 12-month contracts. My preparation paid off and I signed a permanent contract within the first nine months. The other interns were offered temporary extensions, and only one other intern received a permanent employment offer. I blossomed at HPS; the company culture echoed what the website said and work colleagues were more like family, supporting my growth and development. My career at HPS spanned seven years, changing roles on average every two years to more senior positions, starting in the back office and progressing to customer-facing roles. HPS also provided travelling opportunities that allowed me to visit over 100 major cities across 18 countries. Not in my wildest dreams could I have imagined this much travel, each experience bringing new meaning and insight to my life. And in the midst of this jet-setting lifestyle, I pondered, "One day when I'm an old man, will I be sharing quality memories with a soul mate, or would I be alone with shallow memories made up of cheap thrills and temporary highs?"

What happened next set events in motion for me to embark on a Hero's Journey.

27 March 2005, Easter Sunday

My job at HPS entailed working across multiple industries including manufacturing, finance, public sector and telecommunications. With HPS known for printers and laptops, it always came as a surprise to people when I explained that I worked in the enterprise division, designing and building a vast range of complex systems that powered banking transactions, billing systems for telecommunication companies, production systems for a beer manufacturer and the public administration systems used by Home Affairs and the courts. The situation was no different when Mark asked me how to fix an HPS printer at his place of work. "Dude, I work in the enterprise division, not printing," I said to defend my honour. "What does enterprise mean?" he challenged me. While he was my senior by more than a decade, he had been influential throughout my life, convincing me to go back to school when I ran away from home, introducing me to the internet and accompanying me to London for my first international travel. "Give me a business problem?" I dared him, to which he explained. I didn't sleep for two weeks, my mind finally finding a worthy challenge that had the potential to be my claim to fame. Mark worked at Power One, a local utility that provided electricity for areas in the City of Johannesburg. They were using analogue meters and had a challenge collecting revenue from customers: consume electricity first, pay later. Except in their case, payments were seldom made. It wasn't practical or viable, so they explored prepaid meters: pay first, consume only what you paid for. This new model saw revenue collection increase 10-fold while also promoting electricity conservation. The problem: they had several prepaid meter suppliers whose systems were proprietary, meaning they'd have to manage multiple systems and fragmented data streams. They needed one system that could manage all their suppliers and harness the data to optimise their business and operations. I spent the next couple of months visiting Mark after work probing him with question after question. Once I had enough information, I searched the HPS global intranet and stumbled upon an Energy Forum.

Within several hours, a gentleman by the name of Ian replied to my mail; he was the Global Utilities Director.

HPS had the perfect solution, or so we thought. All technology companies lived in an era of speeds and feeds. We received extensive training on product specifications, white papers, product brochures, battles sheets on how to position against competitors, were handed business cards and sent out into the field to sell. I presented our solution to Mark. "Great! – but you need to position it in a way that makes sense. Have a look at our annual reports," he recommended. It felt like the night I started reading Kane and Abel, my head pounding trying to make sense of it all. The close relationship with Mark built over a lifetime meant I could ask all the stupid questions without him losing patience; or to put it more accurately, he couldn't get rid of me. I saw how painful it must have been for customers dealing with our technology-driven approach. Once I got to grips with their financial report, the true nature of the opportunity revealed itself: the way they billed, associated billing losses and its impact on their debtors' age analysis, the cost of disconnects/reconnects, electricity distribution losses and operational expenses like bad debt provisioning. In layman's terms, they were losing hundreds of millions of rands annually. Conversations shifted from technology to business and then from business to social impact. The value realised if the project was implemented meant more people would gain access to electricity. Yes, it was 2005 and many people in disadvantaged areas were still living by candlelight and paraffin heaters.

Mark then explained the ecosystem and stakeholders as a final gesture before stepping back and wishing me luck. From a governance perspective, he could no longer involve himself without compromising his integrity as a public servant. As part of my professional development, management at HPS allowed me to lead the engagement to develop my Account Management skills. Little did any of us know what awaited…

Relationships and trust are everything in sales. They provide the insight to avoid the complexity and politics within organisations, especially when considering that enterprise sales run into tens of millions.

The first meeting at Power One got off to a shaky start. It was my first time leading a presentation to a room of executives, and I was a nervous wreck producing the same broken staccato performance exhibited when losing my virginity. I was failing to impress, and one guy even dropped his head to check his phone. Panic mode. Then a voice in my head as if to calm me said, "Screw it, you've worked too hard on this, you know what to say, speak from your heart!" The tone of the meeting changed. The guy on his phone sat up and took note, even asking a question. "He has already covered that, pay attention!" another executive replied. There was chuckle; I was now in full flow. And just like losing my virginity, once out of the starting blocks, I drove it home to a standing ovation. Two years of preparation and several meetings later, I made it to the CEO. I met Mzingeli aka Thomas at their company staff lunch, a hall filled with a couple hundred people. I had ten minutes to pitch and was competing with the noise that surrounded us. After lunch, he invited me up to his office, confirming interest in our proposal and accepting an invitation to join us at the annual HPS energy conference that was taking place in Monte Carlo – quite an achievement having just met him. 2008 was a year of travel with trips to Romania, the UAE, Istanbul, Monte Carlo and twice to the USA! I was an 'international man of mystery', adding women with exotic accents to my list of conquests.

I first visited Romania in 2007 to spend the European summer with my friend Ionut (Jay) and his girlfriend Ana. Their passion and the longevity of their relationship was something I admired and these two soon married – happy endings were indeed possible. I met Jay when HPS outsourced parts of their operations to an office in Bucharest; it seemed to be the trend for multinationals to leverage cheap labour. I trained Jay as he would support operations in South Africa. Our daily training sessions grew into a friendship and after a visit to SA, I promised to visit him in Bucharest. My first impression of Romania was "What the hell was I thinking!?" There were rows upon rows of concrete matchbox-styled apartment blocks and poor infrastructure that seemed unique to Eastern Europe. Within the first hour my opinion changed, and the people made it one of the best destinations and experiences I've had with their warmth and hospitality, despite the language barrier. The infrastructure and grey buildings grew on me and the only cause for concern was the heat – temperatures reached 43,5 degrees Celsius, causing my body to break out in hives. Of all the places I have travelled to, Romania has the most beautiful women per square kilometre. Even the lady janitor at the airport caught my attention. Its communist history also fascinated me in the similarities with my own struggle. Western Europe viewed Eastern Europe with the same disdain as the apartheid

Chapter 4: Lucky Number Seven

government had viewed people of colour in South Africa. Despite our circumstances, we made the best of it. On a road trip, we passed through Moldova en route to see mud volcanoes. When we stopped at a garage to refuel, Jay turned and said, "Dude, go buy a loaf of bread and a tin of baked beans." "Why," I replied, "Cause that's how you pick up girls here." The laughter that followed hid the contemplative thoughts occupying my mind. White on white hate? White people living in extreme poverty? Perhaps hatred is in the DNA makeup of human beings. Perhaps race had no real significance with financial status or one's ability to generate wealth.

I made it a rule never to visit the same country twice, but when Jay mentioned that Nelly Furtado was performing in their 2008 Bestfest Music Festival, I couldn't miss the opportunity to see my crush perform live. If I wasn't travelling, I'd meet people from other countries visiting South Africa. I had the fortunate opportunity of meeting Sofi, an Australian who was visiting her family, our introduction typical of the many awkward moments in my life. I was exercising in the garage and heard the front gate open, accompanied by chatter and a request for me to come inside. I ignored it to finish the last set of bench press. A flat chest had haunted me my whole life, and I needed to bulk up. Sweaty from the workout, I went inside to find familiar faces and Sofi. She immediately had my full attention: tall, long black hair, fair skin and the biggest dimples you have ever seen. She smiled as she greeted, and her Australian accent had me doing backflips. Calm on the outside, I reached out a hand to welcome her and then laid down on the living room carpet thrusting my hips up in the air in her direction. You can't gym chest and not do abs! It seemed to catch her attention and developed into a romance that had me move out of my parent's home to stay at her apartment. We were inseparable. And while we shared a bed, we never had sex.

Sofi was Christian and practiced celibacy, vowing to save her virginity for marriage. I tested her resolve, but she stood firm and I respected her for it. It was a key moment in my growth, as everything before this was about getting laid. If sex wasn't forthcoming, I'd move on to the next one. Hell, even if sex was forthcoming, I'd move on to the next one. The disappearing act gives birth to the mystery, and the mystery drives attraction – or so I lied to myself. With Sofi it was different. I wanted to stick around, even make time stop as I struggled to come to terms with her pending departure. I had just gotten comfortable falling asleep next to her plus the joys of waking up to somebody, when the reality of her leaving sobered me up. Sofi was on a plane back to Australia and I was back living at my parents' home. Facebook launched in 2004 and took off in South Africa in 2007. I remember listening to the morning drive radio show, sitting in traffic on my way to work, thinking why would anybody want to connect with people online? Yet when the buzz grew I reluctantly signed up. It was strange to connect with people I hadn't seen or spoken to in years, some as far back as primary school.

Reading novels progressed to self-help books, most notable of which was Robert Kiyosaki's Rich Dad, Poor Dad. It reminded me so much of my own circumstances growing up, except I didn't have access to a rich dad. By the time I finished reading the book, the realisation of spending as much money as I was earning and having no assets hit like a blow to the diaphragm. I purchased more books on the topic and attended property seminars. Reading wasn't enough; I needed to act. So in 2007, I co-founded my first company with a relative and bought a property in Gordon's Bay in the Western Cape.

We were making progress on the smart metering opportunity at Power One, but it was still only a side project to my day job and responsibilities at HPS. In January 2008, I was promoted from Pre-sales Consultant to Software Sales Specialist, the accolade of which included a sales conference in Las Vegas. I had a Facebook friend from America, Chloe, who I met via a mutual friend on her visit to Cape Town in 2007. We connected on Facebook and spoke every few months. After sharing the news with her of my trip to Vegas and our plan to visit Los Angeles in November, she replied, "Oh, I have a friend in LA, maybe I could meet you guys there and show you around". Awesome – the best way to travel is with the locals.

Happy days, Sofi was back in SA for a couple weeks, and while we hadn't kept in touch, the chemistry between us was still strong. We spent time together, but this time she was staying at her family's house, so sharing a bed seemed impossible. As the time drew near for her to leave, we grew bold in our attempts to fall asleep together. We were out for supper when I proposed the idea, "Why don't we sneak you into my room?" "Spend the

Chapter 4: Lucky Number Seven

night in your bed, at your parents' house?" she replied, her eyes wide open as she glared at me to gesture, "Are you even serious right now?" "Yes, my parents' morning schedule is like clockwork," I entertained her. "My dad leaves at 6:45 am and my mom leaves at 7:30 am. They never come into my room because I hate being disturbed in the mornings." Sofi had mentioned that the place she was staying at just had a bath, so my final pitch was that she'd be able to shower at our place. Sold!

Thank you HPS Sales Training 101. "Ok," she replied and smiled, accentuating her dimples that had made me fall in love with her.

The thing about living with people your whole life is that you become so accustomed to their ways, the way they think, their habits and behaviour. This predictability gave me confidence that it was possible to get away with Sofi staying the night. My parents were conservative, more so in the sense that my mom worried what the rest of the God-fearing Christian family would think – she was after all their lead spokesperson for many years. As kids, we'd always hear about being "regte mense", Afrikaans for "proper people". The risk was worth taking. The house was dark apart from a side light when we pulled up to the driveway. I jumped out the car to open the gate. If they were still up, the signature sound of our gate would alert them to our arrival. Lights still out, they were asleep. I got back in the car to see Sofi crouched over to avoid being seen. Never mind my parents, we had to stay alert to the nosey neighbours. Once up the driveway undetected, I proceeded back down to close the gate, then back up to the sound of dogs barking to unlock the security gate and front door. It's only through travel that you come to realise how much we live in fear and how this fear translates into big business: security gates, burglar bars, home alarms, car alarms, insurance. But I digress…

The lights were still off as I signalled for Sofi to make her way into the house. "Take off your heels," I whispered as she walked over. She giggled. Inside, she tiptoed behind me to my bedroom. Mission accomplished. We undressed and got into bed. Sofi's clothes lay in a heap next to the bed. The night was peaceful until Sofi let out a faint scream. I had turned and pulled her hair along with me. We lay still, Sofi squeezing my hand expecting us to get caught, but my parents were fast asleep, dead to the night. 5:45 am and I woke to alarm bells going off in my parents' room. Everything went off as I had explained to Sofi over dessert. My dad got showered, had his morning coffee and left for work at 6:30 am. 7:00 am and the TV signalled Mom was up. The sound of running water confirmed she was in the shower. 7:20 am the blow-dryer signalled her location in their bedroom. We were now minutes away from achieving our goal. The reward: the house and shower all to ourselves. I smiled ear to ear as Sofi playfully poked my stomach. The door closed, then the security gate, sounds that were all too familiar. Just then, a car pulled up to our driveway, followed by incomprehensible chatter. I recognised the voice – it was my uncle Alan, but what was he doing at our house so early in the morning? The security gate opened, then the door. They were in the house and our smiles turned to concerned frowns. Footsteps made their way to my parents' bedroom. It was at this point I realised what was going on. We were getting built-in cupboards and the carpenter was here to take measurements and show samples. My room was next. Sofi panicked, "What are we going to do?" "Hide under the sheets as close to me as possible," I whispered as I turned on my left side, my right arm going over my face to block out the morning light. Just then, there was a knock before the door creaked open followed by my mom, uncle and carpenter. "Don't mind him," my mom gestured, "he was out late last night." The carpenter went about taking measurements while giving recommendations about the dimensions and finishings. My mom tried to get my attention, but I pretended to be fast asleep. Sofi laid up against me, undetected. We were just moments away from having the house all to ourselves. Now, my mom had been talking about this for the longest time, so it came as no surprise when she re-entered the room carrying a variety of door handles. "Which one do you like?" she asked with excitement. I ignored her. "Did you drink last night? I hope you weren't drinking and driving? I heard Sofi is in town? Did you guys meet up? This room is stuffy," as she made her way around my bed to open a window. Sofi's clothes still in a heap next to the bed in plain sight, but somehow my mom was none the wiser as she returned to my side of the bed. My arm still over my face, but my eyes now open. Nothing could prepare me for what my mom asked next. "So, did you have sex last night?" Sofi burst out laughing. "What's going on!?" the tone in my mother's voice changed to convey her worst nightmare had just come true. She knew her son had lived in sin for many years, but to bring the sin home was a crime punishable by eviction.

Chapter 4: Lucky Number Seven

Sofi appeared from under the sheets. "Hi Mrs Mooi." My mom blushed as she leaned in to hug her, "I heard you were in the country, good to see you again," before leaving for work. No 'happy shower' as Sofi balked at what people would say. It hadn't reached lunchtime when I received the first phone call. "Heard you got caught," my brother chuckled on the other end as he mocked me for shaming our family. I wasn't too fazed and hoped to get away with just a warning as I strategised on what to tell my father. "It's acceptable in Europe," I'll reason, reminding him of our other brother Lucas' visit when he brought his girlfriend and they shared a bed in our house. My uncle who brought the carpenter couldn't believe that I had a girl under my sheets as he stood there in my bedroom that morning, and the story has since become an urban legend. My dad, upon hearing of the morning's events, said to my mom, "Why Sofi, she is such a sweet girl. Why him of all people?" He was all too aware of my wicked ways and issues with commitment. He was fond of Sofi and thought the world of her. "What are your intentions?" he enquired. "She lives on the other side of the world," I replied. And then, just as we were all excited to have her around, she was on a flight back to Australia.

It was an adventure-filled year. But like a pattern of familiarity that persisted throughout my life, as soon as I found happiness, tragedy would strike. Like the time I had to leave the peace and comfort of my mother's womb, to the devastating pain of changing schools, to the heartbreak and betrayal by Winnie, my grandfather had lost his battle to cancer in February 2008. The nucleus of our family, the man who fixed us when we were sick, who gave us a lifetime of memories affording us holidays at the coast and destinations across South Africa. He was our moral compass, a man I feared and respected. When we were kids, he would send us to the shop, but not before spitting on the floor and telling us to be back before the ground dried. Or the times we had to show him our report cards. One year my report card reflected a 14% average for Maths, to which he enquired, "You got the VAT part, what happened to the rest?" And even when I excelled with 100%, he enquired why I couldn't achieve 110%, the impact still evident today as I am never satisfied. Go against him and he'd have no problem banning and revoking any privileges or support. As we grew older, our relationship changed and there was a softness and openness about him that even saw us engage in banter about my 'sexcapades'. I never knew him to be a religious man as he didn't go to church, never referenced the Bible when teaching us life lessons, and joked that if World War 3 was a religious war, he knew which Muslims he'd kill. I often wondered about his stance on religion seeing that his father was Muslim and his mother a Christian, and when I asked he replied, "My relationship with God is between myself and God, nobody else." The night before he died, there was the familiar haunting sound of water bubbles motioning in his chest as his breath grew shallow. We stood around his bed as his body temperature dropped, his feet and hands cold as his organs shut down and he drew his last breath. It was the most peaceful experience I have ever witnessed, only interrupted by my aunt accusing the Hospice nurse of murdering him for holding his mouth closed to avoid the effects of rigor mortis, another aunt sending out an SMS, "The old man just kicked the bucket". So insensitive I thought. His funeral a testament to the man he was, the church packed inside and out with people travelling from near and far to pay their last respects. At the crematorium, the family gathered at the altar as his casket disappeared into the furnace, tears streaming down their cheeks. I stood wondering why I wasn't able to cry, committing instead to honour his legacy.

An unexpected trip to Germany was on the cards as I had to accompany a client to SAP's headquarters in Waldorf. Company credit card, customer entertainment – until this point I had only lived vicariously through my peers in entertaining customers on international trips. Upon waiting to board a flight from OR Tambo Airport to Germany, I received a text from Sofi, "Which airport are you flying to? I'm in Frankfurt on a layover for 24 hours". She had moved to Abu Dhabi to work as an air hostess. What were the odds? Me hosting a client in Germany, Sofi flying to Germany, both of us at the same airport in Frankfurt. The flight from Johannesburg to Frankfurt is 10 hours 45 minutes, and I couldn't contain my excitement. There was no in-flight entertainment and ample time to think. Thoughts centred on the shower with Sofi that never happened, but this led to some soul-searching questions. It was cheap thrills and temporary highs versus substance and depth. Behind every conquest, there is a story. Growing up in South Africa, there was also the context of race. While I had dismantled prejudices towards other races at an early age, we were still very much sheltered and isolated in our family, communities and social circles. As for superiority/inferiority complexes, sex was just as warped along racial lines. White women were trophies and out of reach. Black women were unattractive, viewed with disdain and were out of the question. "Think about the child's hair and their complexion", and, "What if you catch something" were typical statements made. It disgusted me, but I also wondered if I had held onto certain prejudices. Why didn't I find black women attractive? It bothered me, so when the opportunity presented itself, I tested all the preconceived notions of physical intimacy with different races. Being exposed to different races at a young age dispelled all the ignorant views and prejudices that had shaped my perspective, but could the same be true for physical intimacy? Conclusion: Sex is great regardless of race. Observation: In the white woman's instance, it was a comment, "My grandparents are turning in their graves" that inspired me to go another round and up my performance, while in the black woman's instance, it was the realisation of having an amazing experience. Both encounters shattered any preconceived notions I had held. While great, there was nothing extraordinary about white women. I didn't develop any superpowers, and I saw more and more beautiful black women everywhere I went. Letting go of these misconceptions made me feel free. It's only when you travel to other countries that have long since rid themselves of these oppressive systems that you realise just how powerful and damaging apartheid was in how we were conditioned. Abroad, the race filter wasn't as evident (covert if any) in how they perceived and experienced life, which gave them freedom and opportunities we missed out on because of prejudice. It was upon this realization that I had to confront another issue: objectifying women. Physically, they were all great experiences, but there was no respect and no real substance or depth. The closest I came to an intimate connection was with a person I didn't have sex with, and she was waiting for me at the Hilton Hotel at Frankfurt Airport. Time dragged on as my mind played tricks on me. I vowed to never fly with an airline that had no in-flight entertainment. Our flight landed at 5:20 am. I cleared customs, collected my luggage and rushed to Sofi's hotel room. Excited, I knocked on the door. She opened, wearing only a white gown with the front undone leaving nothing to the imagination. My heart raced. She smiled, her dimples as cute as ever, hugged me and whispered, "You missed your chance to shower with me". I enjoyed this playful nature about our romance; it was fun and wicked at the same time. We chatted for a while before she got into bed. "Hurry and get showered so you can join me." I didn't hesitate and just about rinsed myself off, only to return and find she had already fallen asleep. I snuggled up and watched on as she slept. It baffled me, lying there drifting off to sleep, pondering the connection we shared, yet no sex? We woke up at 2 pm and made our way down for lunch, the conversation dominated by her life as an air hostess, the potential for a long-distance relationship and the acknowledgement that it wasn't practical. We finished our dessert and were going our separate ways again; she was on a flight back to Abu Dhabi and I was on a train to Waldorf. It was the last time we saw each other in person. She moved back to Australia soon after and settled down to start a family of her own. That's the cruel nature of life: you never know when it's the last time you'll see somebody. I wonder if we had known, would we have hugged longer, kissed goodbye with more passion, taken more risks in speaking our minds?

The year flew by and as time grew closer to the sales conference in Las Vegas, my friend Chloe contacted me on Facebook. So many months had passed I forgot about her offer to show us around LA. "Are you guys still coming?" "Yes," I replied, confirming our itinerary.

Growing up on American culture gave more meaning to this trip, but I was cautious about what to expect. A few years prior my brother's visa was rejected twice as high risk that he wouldn't return to South Africa. 9/11 had also changed the world forever. No longer could one go up to the cockpit of a plane, and security and profiling became the acceptable norm. While I didn't face the same scrutiny of Islamic people, I have been questioned at customs as if it was an interrogation. Did the whole world consider us sub-human beings or a threat to Western order? A country who prides itself as being the greatest, built by immigrants and slavery? But I digress…

We flew from Johannesburg via Dakar before stopping in Atlanta and then onto Los Angeles, for a total travel time of 36 hours. In Dakar, security forces woke us up and instructed us to identify our belongings and lift our seats for further inspection. In Atlanta, this paranoia was again evident when luggage security called me over to search my bags. "Sir, step away from the table," he ordered as I leaned in, tired from my travels. He searched my bags wearing surgical gloves and then enquired, "Are you Japanese?" in reference to the order

Chapter 4: Lucky Number Seven

and neatness of my luggage. "I'm OCD," I replied, testing his temperament. Another connecting flight to reach LA as fatigue took over. It was so strange to see people cheer two passengers dressed in military uniform embarking the plane. Killing in warfare could never be just, even if it was in the name of God. Even stranger was the amount of American flags that hung on buildings and homes. Did people need to be reminded of what country they were in? It was noon when we arrived at our motel, sleep deprived and battling jetlag. We consumed a bottle of whiskey to stay awake – it worked! Soon we were off to explore the sights and sounds, helicopters hovering in the distance typical of the paparazzi stalking the wealth of celebrities living in LA. By late afternoon, international roaming kicked in and messages came through on my phone. It was Chloe. "Hey, where are you guys?" She met us with a friend at a restaurant on the Santa Monica promenade, before making our way to a nearby pool hall. As the evening flowed, conversation turned to flirtation. I'm not sure who made the first move, but I am sure of the way the kiss felt: it was different, it left me tingling. We spent the next three days together taking in as much of LA as there was time in the day, visiting universal studios, Santa Monica Pier, Rodeo Drive, Beverly Hills and even a strip club where we shared a lap dance and witnessed the phenomenon of twerking. While wandering the streets of LA, a polite old white lady approached, "What are you?" referring to our ethnicity. Our brown skin and curly hair fascinated her, but it confused her as we were too light to be black and too dark to be white, and we weren't Latino either. There was no formal 'coloured' race in America, where anybody of colour considered themselves black or African-American. It made for interesting conversation and become our lunchtime topic. Chloe considered herself black and had a white dad and black mom; I was fourth generation mixed. Trevor Noah best explains it with his analogy of "concentrate OROS juice and water". It was interesting to note that Chloe felt a sense of belonging as a mixed-race person when visiting coloured communities in SA, whereas I despised the coloured identity and associated stereotypes and found comfort when visiting the USA. Either way, there was no escaping it: even in America, black people identified themselves as "light skin" or "dark skin" African-Americans.

The most notable highlight of our LA trip was bumping into Matt Le Blanc aka Joey from the popular TV series Friends at Carney's in West Hollywood. His signature pickup line "How you doing?" and his way with the ladies made him legendary. We were waiting for our order when he entered. I stood motionless, my brain trying to process what was unfolding. Do I call him Matt or Joey? He nodded as he passed by, and I was still standing motionless as he placed his order. Matt's friend stumbled in after and was so drunk he fell face flat on the floor. We stood starstruck as Matt glanced at his friend with a look of disapproval and then exited to wait in the limo for his order. These LA nights were crazy!

Next stop, Las Vegas! – but not before falling in love. 3 am, a full moon shining light on our naked bodies as we lay on a make-shift bed made of cushions from the living room couch, engaging in conversation and laughter; my heart literally beat so hard and fast that Chloe described it as the whole room shaking, asking me if I could "do it again?" I couldn't. My heart has never raced like that before – was it fatigue from tiredness, or the heart attack my Physical Education teacher had predicted in high school after my childishness to abstain from all sports? We resolved to get some sleep and make the most of our last day together before flying our separate ways. En-route to the airport, we stopped at a Sears' department store, and while the other guys went shopping, Chloe and I stood outside in a warm embrace. My mind flooded with thoughts of her and the moments we had shared, and love washed over me like the wave that knocked me off my feet when visiting the ocean for the first time, leaving me dizzy. My heart was smiling.

We flew into Vegas at night. The runway is parallel to the main strip, and I suspect this is by design and not accidental. It was surreal and somewhat disturbing as we exited the airport to slot machines blasting sounds of coins raining down. A limo awaited us at the arrivals pick-up point, courtesy of HPS, followed by a short ten-minute drive that would create an embarrassing moment if the dashboard camera footage was published. You'd expect four grown men to be speaking about the potential for mischief that Las Vegas presented, but instead our conversation focused on whether the hotel room had enough hangers for our clothing. It was only after mentioning that I travelled with my own hangers, did the driver share that all limos were equipped with dashboard cams after drivers had been victims of assault and even murder by people who had lost money

Chapter 4: Lucky Number Seven

gambling. We checked into the Venetian Hotel and began a week of early mornings and late nights. Keynote speaker Chris Gardner, the entrepreneur behind the biographical drama The Pursuit of Happiness wowed us, there were breakout sessions exposing us to the latest in HPS technologies, and in the evenings, there were gala dinners and the best entertainment that Las Vegas had to offer. After a few days the novelty dissipated and some of the ugly truths were revealed. The casino floors are lost to time, no clocks on the walls and lights dimmed to numb the senses, leaving a person clueless to how long they had been gambling. It was always the same scene whether we went for breakfast, broke for lunch or attended evening dinners. My fascination with the young women accompanying older men led me to Sugar Daddy, a matchmaking site that saw girls from all over America fly in on a Thursday to keep men company, then fly out on Sunday. A visit to a strip club on the outskirts of town showcased women from all over the world, including a lady from Romania. "Che Faci?" I introduced myself, Romanian for "How you doing?" Matt Le Blanc would have been proud. But my heart wasn't in it; it was in Seattle, with Chloe. So I returned to the hotel room instead, went online and hoped she'd be too, which she was. We spoke into the night.

The distance between Johannesburg and Seattle is 16,494 km, the time difference is 10 hours, 9 hours when Daylight Savings. Basic logic and common sense would argue that it was impossible to entertain any idea of romance beyond the three passion-filled days in LA. So we did the impossible – we daydreamed. "Come visit me for Christmas," I tempted her. "Flights are $3000," she replied. There was a slight pause of despondency, "Tickets are only R14,000 for me to visit you." With an exchange rate of 8.25 to the dollar, my flight there was three times cheaper. "So are you coming to visit me Mister Mooi?", to which I replied, "I've already booked my tickets and just emailed you the itinerary".

In the days building up to my visit, two important conversations took place. The first led to us being in an official relationship, my first real relationship, and the other a request for me to get HIV tested. I'd be travelling to Brazil in January and needed to get a yellow fever injection, so the plan was to get the vaccination and be tested before flying out. But once at the clinic, I freaked out. I had practiced safe sex religiously but became haunted by all the conquests. Also, the results would only be available after five days due to the method of testing.

So when the nurse warned about getting a vaccination and the risk of a compromised immune system, I came to make the stupidest and most reckless decision of my life: I took the yellow fever injection but not the HIV test, then lied and said I did.

I flew via Amsterdam to Seattle to avoid the two-hour stopover in Dakar. No problems this time at customs or baggage claims as I exited to the arrivals section, taking an escalator to find Chloe waiting for me. She stood in a blue jeans and green hoodie, her hair curly; a memorable moment which took 26 hours, 16,836 km across 10 time zones to create. We stayed at Chloe's apartment in the University of Washington district. Her meticulous planning made it a jam-packed trip of adventure as we took in all the sights and sounds Seattle had to offer, The Space Needle, seeing Mos Def AKA Yasiin Bey live at the Moore Theatre, Pike Place Market, seeing the legendary Roots live at the Paramount Theatre, Starbucks' first ever store and Alki Beach. Seattle is a gem of a city surrounded by water, mountains and evergreen forests, made extra special by the amount of snow which fell that year. At 29 years of age, I experienced snow for the first time, building a snowman after getting drunk at Earl's Pub in the university district on Long Island iced teas. At night, we'd lay in bed and I would stare out the window in amazement at the snow falling and the reddish tinge of the night sky, while resuming my childhood habit of playing with Chloe's ears. Was it the cold weather that kept her ears cool, or the way her body regulated her temperature? We travelled to Quinault Resort and Casino, two hours out of Seattle on the Pacific Northwest for a few days to experience snow on the beach, such a contrast to what I experienced back home on the south coast of the Indian ocean. A place I will always remember; it was the location where Chloe first told me she loved me, a sentiment I shared and didn't hesitate in reciprocating. We also took a drive up to Bellingham, one and a half hours north of Seattle to have lunch with an old friend from Sacred Heart College. Nicholas had immigrated to Canada the same year I changed schools. It was great to reminisce about our boyhood friendship. We then flew to Spokane for Christmas, her hometown to the east of Washington State where I'd "Meet the fockers".

Chapter 4: Lucky Number Seven

The plane descended as it snowed and it was magical, as if we were inside a snow globe. After years of disappointing Christmas gifts, I received a gift I could finally use: a goodie bag of sex toys from Chloe's parents. We returned to Seattle to bring in the New Year at a house party, waiting for the fireworks display from the Space Needle before calling it a night; I had a morning flight home. It had been such an amazing three weeks, so leaving her was a bitter pill to swallow, only made easier in that we'd be seeing each other in the coming weeks. She agreed to join us in Rio, Brazil.

The decision to celebrate my 30th birthday in Rio was not random. My parents honeymooned there 35 years earlier, taking a 30-day cruise on the Reina Del Mar from Cape Town to Rio. This trip was special for so many reasons. Notably, I could cover all my parents' travel expenses. Chloe's vibrant personality won over my family and prompted a trip for her to visit SA in the coming months. And while love was in the air, we ignored the warning signs that our relationship had some serious hurdles to overcome. Our love was a passionate affair, and our limited time together added a layer of intensity that overwhelmed most people – we loved hard and we fought hard. She was vocal, and I knew what buttons to push to set her off. My most powerful weapon – ignoring her. The tropical climate of Brazil confirmed an earlier question I had pondered: Chloe's ears did in fact remain cool, even in the warm weather.

In Rio, we stayed in a four-bedroom apartment on the 7th floor in Copacabana, our room overlooking the manicured white beaches where we'd wake to the most beautiful sunrises. It was an action-packed trip, sightseeing during the day and passion-filled love-making sessions at nights. Rio is a traveller's paradise, its scenic landscape among the most beautiful on the planet. Cable cars to the summit of Sugarloaf Mountain, helicopter rides over the city, visits to Mount Corcovado where the Christ the Redeemer statue stands 38m tall overlooking Rio, the legendary Maracanã Stadium – home of Brazilian soccer, Sambadrome – featuring parade floats of the Carnaval festival, Samba School practice sessions with Portella which made for an entertaining evening – flamboyant costumes and samba dancers mirrored to the city's vibrant personality, the beautiful bodies and scrumptious food – coconut water, prawn skewers, mojitos, espitada buffets found on Ipanema and

Copacabana beaches, island hopping day trips and a visit to the Favela Da Rocinha to affirm that there is poverty and inequality in paradise, even with Christ watching over.

And here I was, 30 years old and sharing a bed with my girlfriend, or as the 'regte mense' would say, living in sin. Chloe wasn't religious and preferred to identify as spiritual. Our only reference to God was right before she orgasmed. Either way, my parents gave their blessing, and that's all that mattered. Their world views had changed and weren't as conservative like when we were younger, a noticeable shift from the traditional dogma towards one of openness and mutual respect.

As far as passion-filled love-making sessions went, there were still items from our Christmas gift that included his-and-her candy underwear, lube, edible paints, scented candles, massage oils, mints, an assortment of condoms and a super-powered vibrating ring – a bullet mounted on a silicone ring for the ultimate intimate experience and mutual satisfaction. Our souls connected, a love likened to the ocean, deep and dangerous. Our minds lost, possessed by the same ocean, our bodies moved like waves crashing on the beach. We were adventurous in our expression of love, inhibitions swept away like the ocean's strong undercurrent.

Our long-distance romance included trips to Cairo, Alexandria and Sharm el Sheikh in Egypt, road trips from Seattle to San Francisco, and on other occasions from Ann Arbor to San Francisco, Ann Arbor to Chicago, and visits to Cape Town and Durban in SA. It was an adventure-filled holiday romance, the stuff of romantic movies: different cultures, exotic locations and impossible circumstances (exchange rate, work, money, time difference) to overcome. And while my weapon of choice was ignoring her, Chloe's was breaking up. It was Winnie all over again. She grew frustrated and wanted to end things. She fought with me because I was quiet at the dinner table. In comparison, Americans sure were loud in restaurants. For us though, it was quiet time. When our family got together, it sounded like a war zone bombarded by noise, but when people sat down to eat, dead silence. From my side, it was the anger of never feeling appreciated for financial matters. No matter what I did, it was as if there was always a sense of expectation. It

Chapter 4: Lucky Number Seven

drove me to silence, which only intensified our fighting. Chloe even fought with me for not proposing to her when she visited my family in South Africa! Then there was tension between our business versus social outlooks. As a social science major, Chloe always challenged my business ideas for their lack of empathy towards people; my stance on profit somewhat invalidating everything she stood for. The longer the relationship lasted, the more vested we became, making it harder to let go. In spite of our dysfunction, we persisted and things appeared to get easier as we grew as individuals and as a couple. Her passion for social impact started to influence my approach towards business. And while romance was blossoming, a promising career at HPS was coming to an end.

The first significant blow was when the lady from HR sent out a spreadsheet to the countrywide mailing list by accident, containing the pension and provident fund details for all employees, exposing our salaries. By the time she or management had realised what had happened, I was among the staff who had opened the attachment, using my Microsoft Excel skills to create a pivot table that revealed the highest and lowest paid employees, and where I stood against my peers. It was a Pandora's Box which disclosed that my salary was R20,000 per month less than any of my peers. Within minutes, another email warning staff of disciplinary action for opening or discussing the spreadsheet, but it was too late – my blood was boiling. How could I get up and go to work knowing what I knew? I confronted my manager and discovered my salary was a result of the base pay of my first employment contract, the internship. Salary reviews meant I'd have to wait three or four cycles to achieve parity with my peers. I had closed the biggest software sales deal for Q1 in FY2009, so my manager agreed to help fast track the process. No pay increase was forthcoming however, as the new Middle East and Africa regional structure based out of Dubai worked to fire her before she could bring parity to my salary situation. Their ruthless actions, a noticeable shift from the familiar family culture. Little did I know I was also on their hit list. Perhaps accusing them of being short-sighted on the big deal closed in Q1 wasn't in my best interests, but I always put customers first.

The next significant blow related to the smart metering deal at Power One. The pet project to aid in my professional development had grown into a multimillion dollar opportunity, $71,106,240.00; or, at an exchange rate of 14,49, a billion-rand opportunity R1,030,258,311.36, a number president Zuma would struggle to read out loud. I wonder if the architects of apartheid had anticipated a "Jacob Zuma" one day becoming our country's first citizen, would they still have followed through with their plans of segregation and oppression – an inferior education? Probably not. Go read the Willie Lynch letter "The making of a slave", written on December 25th, 1712 to understand how these architects have shaped our society, sharing fool proof methods for controlling black slaves, which if correctly installed would last 300 years! But I digress again…Alarm bells were going off at HPS HQ in the USA; the deal had gotten the attention of the highest office. Questions ranged as to the validity of the deal and my involvement. Management eventually sent a close friend and mentor to deliver the bad news: they were removing me from the deal and assigning it to somebody more "senior". It wasn't the first time either, I was blocked from going to Monte Carlo the previous year, only for Thomas, the CEO at Power One, to ignore all their calls, and only after his refusal to attend the conference if I was not present did they approve my travel. While I was understanding of their decision from a corporate perspective, I grew anxious as to whether they'd even compensate me for what would be the biggest single deal in the country's history. Anxiety was ever-present in my emotions, developments or setbacks on the deal could make or break my day.

To recap, the deal started off as a technology discussion that progressed into a business and social impact conversation which the proposal, after years of work, now reflected. HPS had a global financial services division that could loan Power One R1,030,258,311.36 at a fixed 4% interest rate, which would allow them to roll out prepaid meters to all homes in their area of supply. Power One would use the HPS smart metering solution and services to maximise revenue collection and pay back the loan. It was genius. We structured the deal as an unsolicited bid for a loan and not as a technical solution, which would be subject to a tender process. Our team met to complete the offer prior to meeting Thomas for dinner later that night, a proposal he would present at the mayoral committee meeting the following day. I looked at the

Chapter 4: Lucky Number Seven

offer and noted the interest rate was 5.80% as opposed to the 4%. "Let's have room to negotiate, we can't go in on our best offer," said the finance guy, to which I argued, "This is not one of those deals", only for our CEO to pull rank, "We go with 5,80%". I persisted and was told, "Know your place". It's a 20-minute drive from Rivonia to Sandton, but that day of all days took more than an hour, perhaps a sign of how long it would take for the deal to close. We met Thomas and presented him with the proposal. He flipped past the first eight pages in haste and looked up at me when he reached page nine after seeing the 5,80%. Thomas confirmed what I had been arguing earlier: anything higher than 4% meant no deal. Our CEO then delivered his signature line which we mocked him for. "Thomas, I give you my word we will have a proposal with 4% to you by the morning." "I give you my word..." was confirmation that a revised proposal would not be forthcoming, and that's exactly what happened. The mayoral committee meeting motioned for the unsolicited bid to go to tender and we lost all advantage. I was accused of not knowing the customer and placed on a performance review.

It was around this time I met Arthur, tasked to help the new member of the software team settle in. We went for lunch and within a couple hours, Arthur convinced me to leave the corporate world with a vision of greater purpose.

A month into my performance review and I was miserable. Management was out to see me leave, deploying the same ruthless tactics they used to remove my previous manager. But as they were building their case, I reciprocated by preparing a case to expose them. And so when my manager called me in to complete the retrenchment process, I reminded him of the software deal we closed in Q1. I was away in Brazil for the last week in January, and they had seen to all the paperwork.

When I accused them of being short-sighted, it was in response to a complaint I received from the client. Upon investigating, I discovered that they contravened revenue recognition rules so that the deal could be included in the first quarter results, a serious offense under global governance as HPS was a listed company. I had already typed out an email to corporate governance exposing my manager and the regional management team in Dubai. "Send it," he said, calling my bluff. I left the meeting room and walked with pace back to my desk like a soldier marching into battle, but before I could get there, my manager called again, this time pleading the opposite. Regional management agreed to pay a severance package, I accepted their offer, and so finished a seven-year spell at HPS. What a lucky and privileged seven-years it had been. How different would my life be had I not secured the internship? If work ethic was anything to go by, I was the last person to leave the office. While my colleagues went for afternoon drinks to signal the end of another sales quarter, I stayed behind to complete work due to clients.

After handing in my equipment, the reality of what was happening kicked in. It was surreal. I felt scared, excited, and didn't know what to expect. I saved up enough money to keep me afloat for a while and knew the Power One deal was real; it was just a matter of time, the financial returns were enough to last two life times, a risk worth taking. Not being tied down to a 9–5 with 21 annual leave days also gave me the freedom to spend more time in the USA.

Little did I know I had answered my Call to Adventure. It was a moment likened to the scene from the hit movie, The Matrix. Take the blue pill and wake up to the comforts and security of a steady income, medical aid, cell phone, petrol and car allowances, company travel, awesome commissions, a career. Or take the red pill and see how deep the rabbit hole goes...

CHAPTER 5

HOW DEEP DOES THE RABBIT HOLE GO?

Chapter 5
HOW DEEP DOES THE RABBIT HOLE GO?

I founded Marvel Technologies in November 2009 and then flew out to America to spend a month with the love of my life, who had now moved across country to Ann Arbor in Michigan to do her honours in Social Work. Upon arrival I met her roommate, Eric. While I should have been concerned about my girlfriend sharing an apartment with another man, Eric was no ordinary man; he was transgender. Born female, she transformed into a male by hormone therapy and removing her breasts. The only reason to be jealous: Eric had more facial hair than me. The only thing more confusing at the time was that Eric identified as a gay man. It came as no shock when Bruce Jenner transformed into Caitlyn in 2015. The other standout event was attending a party where I'd meet fellow expat Ray, whose family had immigrated many years back from Cape Town to Ann Arbor. It turned out my good friend Arthur had stayed with their family when he attended college there. What were the odds!?

Chloe confronted me for being too quiet again during lunch at a fancy Italian restaurant. My quietness was different this time however, as I had no job to go back home to and my future was uncertain. I kept quiet to avoid panic and didn't want to burden her with my problems. What was I thinking, earning rands, spending dollars? It didn't make any sense!

I returned to the USA in April again to see Chloe graduate, a memorable occasion that saw President Barack Obama deliver the commencement speech, addressing some 3,500 undergraduates and a crowd 85,000 strong. It was a proud moment; and at 24 years of age, Chloe aspired to complete her PHD before turning 30. We then embarked on a seven-day road trip that saw us cover 2,632 miles (4,237 km) passing through 10 states to reach San Francisco where Chloe was interning for the summer. Of all my visits, this trip was the most unpleasant. Our fighting persisted and Chloe evoked

Chapter 5 : How Deep Does the Rabbit Hole Go?

another break up. I didn't know anybody else and my return tickets were from San Francisco, which was still two weeks away. Homesickness set in and my lingering quietness only made Chloe more furious. We were out of options, so I had no other choice but to talk, telling her what I was going through and the things I didn't like about our relationship. It calmed her and brought peace to our union.

I returned home after a 30-hour flight to life as an entrepreneur and was off on another 8-hour flight to Dubai the very next day to attend the annual HPS Energy Conference, flights and accommodation courtesy of HPS. In the build-up to leaving HPS, I mentioned my situation to Thomas – we had built up a relationship of personal trust and honour over corporate gamesmanship. He offered to mentor me as the lead architect of the smart metering deal as an independent company, provided I had the support of HPS to deliver if we won the tender. I imagine it left a bitter taste in the mouths of those at HPS who had thought they'd seen the last of me, but my relationships and supporters were at a global level.

In the time it took for the tender to be released, I would live ten lifetimes, learn to stop time and also remember the future. Inspirational and thought-provoking quotes became a way of life.

CHAPTER 5
REHAB

Chapter 6
REHAB

*"Can you remember who you were, before the
world told you who you should be?"*
~ Danielle LaPorte

It was time to journal again, creative writing an outlet to capture the thoughts of trying to make sense of life.

'We come into a world born with no choice and no memories. Amnesia. Our gender, names, religion, spoken languages, race and financial status all predetermined. Our lives and beliefs shaped by those closest to us — our parents, family, friends, community and country. We go through life, expected to conform and obey without question, protected by those who love us from the harsh realities of the outside world with little white lies and used by those who seek to forward their purpose with forces unknown. We are dispensable, going through life sedated and blinded by our privilege, limited by our perceptions and crippled by our fear. We're indifferent to anything and anyone that doesn't fit the mould. We praise and seek favour, but stay stuck in misery and suffering rather than venture into the unknown in pursuit of the truth and happiness, keeping others down with us. We marvel at our superiority and ability to reason while ignoring how similar we are to cancer and parasites.'

As time went by, I realised that I had no freaking clue what I was doing! At corporate, I had a role that came with a job spec and responsibilities, a companywide team with global reach to support me and a hierarchical management structure that led and managed the business. HPS was a brand so trusted that all it required was handing out a business card at meetings to gain a client's confidence. At Marvel Technologies, it was just myself and Arthur, who was still full time at HPS. I offered him equity in exchange for helping me build the business. I had no personal brand, no reputation

Chapter 6: Rehab

to speak of, why would anybody trust me, let alone do business with me? So what did I do? I got us business cards. Low budget, so it had both our names on it, only to discover a spelling error after printing 500: it read Marvel "Technolgies". Go Slow! Mistakes, setbacks and rejections formed part of a narrative that was "FML" or "WTF".

It was a time of discovery; opportunity would find me and failure would shape me.

On one occasion I attended a tender briefing. "What do I need to do?" I enquired, wanting to earn my stripes. "Just make sure you sign the register." I arrived, signed the register and found a spot in the corner of the room, standing against the wall, notepad in hand, but taking no notes. Instead, I observed how people were so caught up in taking notes and asking questions that they didn't notice me standing up against the wall. Unknown to them, a deal was already done and the briefing session was just a formality. I thought back to all the times I took notes and prepared proposals for done deals. It was an important realization – I didn't want to be a pawn in the thriving world of tenderpreneuring, or build a business that compromised my integrity. I withdrew all contact and shifted my energy elsewhere.

Plenty more insights followed, such as where and how much money I was wasting, buying things I didn't need or use, and what I was doing with my time. It led me to a rule I still live by today – design your life to go against the traffic. The other realisation – I couldn't recall the last time I was sick. Significant, considering I suffered with seasonal flu and post nasal drip my whole life.

Working from home also brought a quietness that allowed me to think and ask pertinent questions like: Who am I? What do I want to achieve? Who do I want to be? How was I going to close those gaps? Days and nights were filled reading autobiographies, self-help and business books.

A week before the 2010 FIFA World Cup, an HPS colleague contacted me; his wife worked for a production company and wanted me to fly to LA and straight back to pick up a green screen. Back to back 23h05m flights would put off even the most enthusiastic traveller, so I proposed they consider flying Chloe from San Francisco to LA, for her to collect the equipment, and then fly to SA and spend a week here before flying back home. They agreed, so it was just a matter of getting Chloe on board. What were the odds!? This was the crazy nature of our long-distance relationship and there was no hesitation from her side, apart from getting off work. Thirty-six hours later and Chloe landed in Johannesburg. South Africa was a different place during the World Cup. It was in a celebratory mood that had everybody drunk with soccer fever, forgetting their problems for a month. Chloe was only here for one week, but that's all it took to convince her to move permanently to South Africa.

She finished her internship in San Francisco and arrived back in SA to her new life on September 29th 2010, my late grandfather's birthday. After two years of jet-setting, we were finally living in the same place and time zone. A reality that had me feeling both excited and concerned, I was thrilled at her courage to take action and give our relationship the best chance of succeeding, but also concerned as to what lay in store, since we often overlooked the small details, like our different lifestyles. In the US, we were always on the move. In SA, we spent most of the time at home or with family. I was over my clubbing phase and was disciplined in keeping to a budget, all issues that Chloe raised concerns over. She was giving up everything to move to SA and it wasn't just a matter of weeks to get through.

Alain, a car guard at the gym I attended, brought his family to South Africa from the DRC in the hope of a better life. A qualified economics major, he worked for three years "looking after" cars, with no formal salary except for tips, all because he didn't have the proper paperwork. During the xenophobic attacks in 2010, he was so desperate for the safety of his family, he handed out a letter to the people whose cars he guarded. I contributed the first R50, and after one month he had raised R1,000. During all that time, he never once complained about his plight, and always asked about my dad; they shared the same name, 'Allen'. So one day after gym, reversing out of the parking lot as he directed me, I rolled down the window and handed him a tip, the remaining R1,500 he needed. It was the first time I helped somebody and had nothing to gain, no expectations and no need for praise. It was a defining moment for Alain too. Three weeks later, he and his family got their

Chapter 6: Rehab

papers just as a vacancy opened at a factory that needed a French-speaking foreman. He got the job. What were the odds!?

The first couple of months with Chloe were blissful, a honeymoon of sorts that saw us apply for life partner permits. We slept in late, ate out for lunch, went for couples' massages, outings and dinners – repeat. Business took a backseat as I poured all my energy into making sure my lover settled comfortably into her new environment. She was my muse, my inspiration and supporter, she understood my ambitions and wasn't fazed by the struggle and sacrifices that came with it. My parents allowed us to 'live in sin' at our house without judgement. For Chloe, who like many Americans had left home after finishing school and lived in her own apartment while at university, it took getting used to. In December, I surprised her with a trip down to Durban for her 25th birthday. The celebrations were short-lived as a huge argument ensued to unveil a doomed romance. Chloe had a pending student loan to pay back, living only off what financial support I provided and what her dad sent her. For somebody who had thrived on freedom and independence, she was frustrated and trapped in isolation where everything was on my terms – my family, my friends, my car, my home, my money. Her only control and power – sex. I sensed a change in the dynamics of our intimacy. It was a downward spiral of despair and hopelessness causing her to break down in tears. I had no answers and tried to console her, assuring her that everything was going to be ok – but it wasn't. The Power One tender would be out soon and the financial pressures that appeared to be the source of our restrictive lifestyle and unhappiness would cease, ignoring more pressing concerns. As the weeks went by, her depression grew. It must have been torture for somebody as smart and vibrant as her to watch reruns of Will & Grace and play SIMS all day. I was taking serious strain too but said nothing. So, as I waited for the tender to be released, Chloe looked for jobs back home – she wanted to go back to university. Like on so many other occasions where the universe was conspiring, she secured an interview with a company from her hometown. They were so impressed, they offered to pay for her flights back to the US for a second interview. What were the odds!? I was relieved, thinking we could resume our long-distance relationship, free to handle our business, and work towards an alternative way forward. Chloe reached a different conclusion. She returned home on March 11th, 2011 and ended the relationship soon after, leaving me heartbroken. Accepting this fate was beyond me and I embarked on a doomed quest to resurrect our relationship, my efforts relentless; a downward desperate spiral that had me implode to experience the worst pain and darkness of my life. March 25th, 2011 – Death announced itself via Facebook for the first time. A friend from primary school died in a car accident, leaving behind his wife and three young kids. It left me wondering why death didn't take me instead. He had everything to live for, I had nothing.

Looking back and reflecting on this time, death did visit me: it was the death of my ego.

CHAPTER 7

THERE ARE FAR WORSE THINGS THAN DEATH

Chapter 7
THERE ARE FAR WORSE THINGS THAN DEATH

Breakups were easier in the not-so-distant past. Apart from a few shared friends, people would grow apart and move on with life. In a new world of social media, Facebook meant you were still in each other's lives, along with everybody else. I was in such a state of rage I unfriended Chloe and deleted every picture we had ever taken together, deactivating my profile to avoid accepting what was going on. Chloe said she loved me and respected me, but wasn't in love with me. She wanted to stay friends. And when I argued, Chloe accused me of being passive aggressive, and said she could no longer deal with my anger. "What do you mean passive aggressive?" I reacted, not knowing what she meant. A Google search provided more information. It was humbling; I was indeed passive aggressive. There is something ghostly about discovering things that were previously unknown and limited to my subconscious. To prove my willingness to grow and be the man she needed me to be, I reflected and kept a journal of the recommended exercises to help overcome this anger. I shared it with her and for a moment it felt as though she might reconsider. But by the fifth reflection, the authenticity of my writing was undone by the desperate attempt to resurrect our relationship. She stood firm and felt I was trying to manipulate her. And so continued my downward spiral into the darkness. I lost 12 kilograms in a matter of weeks, a fist length between my pants and waist, my face gaunt-looking as if I had been in a concentration camp. Depressed and lost in sorrow, it was only after my parents confronted me that I realised the state I was in. I stopped going to the places we frequented and my only solace become a torture chamber. Winter was arriving, and it was the season my family took up building 5,000-piece puzzles while listening to hit music from the different eras, their tough love stance ever-present as they did custom voice-overs for songs on the playlist. The 1977 hit by Player, 'Baby come back' became 'Chloe come back'. And when opportunity presented itself, they went onto Facebook and spoke about what Chloe had been up to. They knew exactly

Chapter 7: There are Far Worse Things than Death

which buttons to push to set me off. I resumed digital scrapbooking and used my Photoshop skills to create a collage using pictures from our time together to form a marriage proposal. I even called her dad to ask for his blessing, which he gave but advised to give her space and to check in once a month. If anybody knew her, he did, so I followed his advice. But devastating news soon reached of her new-found romance and happiness. My body ached all over – I'd never experienced physical and emotional pain like this. Lying in bed, I ran my fingers through the corners of what was once her pillow, imagining it was her ear. I felt every single atom in my body aching and continued losing weight, this time the gap two fists between my pants and waist. An emotional trauma with no release was building.

My suffering was evident for all to see, so my brother decided a night out was just the intervention needed. Sushi king Kenny Kunene spent at least R20 million on a disastrous three-city ZarFest tour. We attended the Johannesburg leg that included superstars Timbaland, Ciara, Lil' Kim, Phat Joe and DJ Scratch. But instead of enjoying the concert, I got drunk off red wine after chatting to Chloe on MSN messenger. On the drive home, my pent-up emotion exploded into a river of tears that streamed down my face. It was so emotional, my brother's girlfriend cried as she tried to console me. Jonathan, instead, turned and said, "Must I put you out of the car? We don't cry in our family!" He was right, we didn't. I hadn't cried since childhood. There was even 'rust in my tears' we joked to break the awkward silence that ensued.

The tears, inspiration for a poem she would never get to hear.

Indigo Child

Random events... infinite possibilities, one choice...
He said she said... emotions be driving, logic called shotgun...
Me, myself & I plus the occasional hitchhiker, destination unknown...
Blink my eyes, the scene changes, blink, blink, blink, how will I ever find my way back home...
Blinded by the light, inspired by the darkness...
Stubborn and dedicated,
we might just get it to work in spite of ourselves and what others say...
Love, it was just a game we played!
Look forward, never look back, consumed by anger,
Have I made the right decisions, pride won't let me say...
Success is inevitable, motivated by the pain...
I'm on that 80:20 grind, what to do with all this time...
Some grow old, some grow young... no respect for the rules, it's all relative, anyway...
Time to stand up, time to shine...
Time travel, will you be mine...
13,661 km, 8489 miles away, but distance isn't the only thing that stands in our way...
Broken promises, we'll make up for it someday...
One day, when our words and actions mean the same thing...
Until then, I'm married to the game, giving birth to ideas...
But will it be the same?

Chapter 7: There are Far Worse Things than Death

And true to her father's word, I'd hear from Chloe once a month. Nothing more than, "Hi, how are you? Gotta run". My only distraction, the release of the Power One smart metering tender.

I contacted HPS with the good news and they agreed to support me; they would lead the bid and Marvel Technologies would deliver services to form part of a black economic empowerment and job creation value proposition – I wasn't a fan of BEE and preferred being selected on merit as opposed to the colour of my skin. We had a month to submit our proposal, but it wasn't the usual chaos and tight deadlines associated with a tender response as we had already done most of the work.

It was around this time that the Limpopo Textbook Crisis made headlines for the non-delivery of textbooks to schools. I wasn't a fan of the news and brushed it aside, thinking they should just digitise textbooks and give every learner a tablet PC.

With two weeks to go, I checked in with HPS, but they were unresponsive and not taking calls. I contacted Thomas, who had left Power One to pursue personal interests in wind energy, while staying true to his word to mentor me. "Try regional management," he recommended. So I reached out to Ian, the Global Utilities Director with whom I had established a relationship years earlier, and who had flown to SA upon my request for him to speak at a local energy conference. Ian's voice eluded that something was wrong and he soon shared the news that HPS had decided not to submit a bid. "Why?" It baffled me. Ian shared details of an internal meeting in which local management decided it wasn't worth pursuing because "they had been burnt in the past". I thanked Ian for all his support, wished him well and, by the time the call had ended, I had moved on. No regrets, no hate, no anger. I was going to make a name for myself in the education sector by solving the textbook crisis.

Power One awarded the R1,25 billion smart metering tender several months later. Looking back and reflecting on this time, the death of my ego brought with it my rite of passage to selflessness.

CHAPTER 8

That One Time I Stopped Time

Chapter 8
THAT ONE TIME I STOPPED TIME

Upon embarking on a Hero's Journey and answering one's Call to Adventure, mentors and guides mysteriously appear. My situation was no different.

Arthur sent me a link which opened to Stanford University's postgraduate E145 course: the Fundamentals of Technology Entrepreneurship taught by the legendary Steve Blank. Stanford University is a leading research and teaching institution in California, USA. The chances of me getting in, let alone affording it were zero. Steve Blank is a Silicon Valley serial-entrepreneur and academician who pioneered the Customer Development Methodology which launched the Lean Start-up movement. The website was open to browse, and I could access course material and presentations made by students. I sourced the reading material and then followed week by week as the course unfolded, applying what I had learnt to discover my calling – to help improve the quality of education outcomes. The smart metering opportunity had taken years to piece together; this new venture in education took but a month. Business Model Generation was a game changer that shifted my focus from 'let's give every kid a tablet PC' to creating true value that would have a significant impact on teaching and learning outcomes. I was so immersed and present in my attention and effort, I managed to stop time. The mountain of researching, strategising, discovery and validation, and tactical planning all completed and ready for execution with three days to spare of my October 31st deadline. I had even forgotten about the pain and heartbreak that had been haunting me for months. I was getting my life in order and went for the HIV test. It came back negative.

Chloe and I spoke at length for the first time since our break-up. We engaged in banter and the conversation flowed. She even told me she found herself playing with her ear, which made her think of me.

Chapter 8: That One Time I Stopped Time

I realised that I was still very much in love with her while accepting that she had moved on. Panic set in and short-circuited the neural network that coordinated activities between my brain and fingers to send her an email. The email, a list of confessions designed to provoke animosity, ensuring she'd never want to speak to me again. I had to protect my fragile heart. Among it, confessing that I didn't go for the HIV test two years earlier, not mentioning my negative status either. It worked. She raged and vowed never to speak to me again, ever. It was a relief; like the schoolboy who told his parents, "It's no loss", at least now I didn't have to wait to have our once-a-month conversations. A week later I was on a flight to America.

The E145 course introduced concepts of leverage and on-demand staff: if there's somebody who can do it better and cheaper than you, partner with them. With the business plan formulated, I searched the internet and found a company headquartered in California who were already far down the line on a solution that matched my business requirements – content aggregation and single sign-on. I prepared a business proposal using the business model canvas and sent it off to their CEO. It was a Sunday. I recall hesitating whether to send it or wait until Monday, but came to the realisation that if he was a CEO like me, days of the week didn't matter. I was right. Robert replied within two hours, complimenting me on a sound business proposal, as well as an invite to meet him in London. He'd be there for a week and could see me for an hour. "An hour?" I pondered, as I weighed up the costs, travel time and visa application. "Would it not be better for me to spend a week with you at your headquarters in California?"

Upon touching down in America, it was strange to imagine a visit to the US without Chloe being the reason. Should I contact her? I felt the pain of her absence when exploring the streets of San Francisco, my favourite city. At the tourist attractions were ghostly remnants of a happier past where we had once made priceless memories. It cut through me like a blade. The pain felt different though, I had found a purpose that was greater than us, greater than myself. So I put on a brave face and went to meet my new friend, Robert. I spent the week meeting his team, learning more about their company and negotiating a partnership agreement. In my leisure time, I explored the Bay Area and took part in the Occupy Wall Street protests. At night, Robert and his family hosted me for dinner. His wife worked at HPS and knew the Research & Development team I had worked with on the Power One deal. In our time architecting the smart metering deal, we also explored cutting-edge nano-technology that could combat cable theft, another billion-rand problem that needed solving. What were the odds!? It made for great conversation. On other occasions, I wandered the streets of San Francisco alone, drinking at the pubs along the pier to ease my sorrows, before returning to the hotel room where I noticed that the same infomercial was playing on the telly. This guy Shaun T claimed to have created the toughest workout ever, calling it 'Insanity'.

I returned home to SA with renewed energy and focus. Growing from strength to strength, my learning curve seemed exponential as I immersed myself in learning how to run a business, understanding legal jargon, accounting, marketing, and engaging with a multitude of stakeholders and organisations in the basic education sector. The most significant aspect of my growth was finding a way back to God.

Nevertheless, tension grew between myself and Arthur. Expectation left me frustrated, compounded by a sense of unwanted obligation on his part. Arthur arranged for us to meet with some elderly businessmen who had an extensive network that could give us access to senior government officials. The cost: they wanted to lead the engagement under their brand, rendering us employees. I wasn't having it. My reluctance to entertain any discussions angered Arthur, who accused me of being immature and stubborn. Paranoia kicked in – was I getting screwed? I was the one who developed the business proposal, flew to the USA and secured the partnership, now these old men wanted to reimburse my travel expenses to justify them owning the venture? Paranoid thoughts escalated with me serving Arthur 'divorce papers'. As a close friend and business partner, it was the most difficult decision I've had to make. We had embarked on an entrepreneurial journey when nobody quite knew what entrepreneurship was – we couldn't even explain it ourselves. It had been a lonely journey and to lose somebody like Arthur was devastating. The 'divorce' had the opposite effect though – we grew closer. I was so scared to go it alone that I didn't even think about what Arthur had wanted when he shared his vision of greater purpose. I roped him in with no consideration,

Chapter 8: That One Time I Stopped Time

then felt disappointed when my expectations weren't being met. Free of expectation and given the room to live our individual dreams, we continue to support each other and grow our reputations as social change mavericks.

Introspection of "who I was", "who I had become", and "who I wanted to be" was as integral as the air I breathed. "How much do you want to succeed? What are you prepared to give?" I now understood what commitment meant; I wanted to succeed so badly even if it meant the death of me, losing my fear of the unknown and unfamiliar in the process. Mentally, I was reading every day and working towards mastery. Physically, I was exercising three days a week and needed to do more, recalling the infomercial that played in the hotel room in San Francisco. I sourced a copy and started the Insanity workout on December 31st 2011, Chloe's favourite day of the year. It was the most challenging fitness programme ever created. A 60-day total body workout based on a fitness method called 'max interval training'. It maxes your heart rate for three minutes with only 30-second rest intervals in between, burning up to 1,000 calories within an hour. It was a day I'll never forget as I completed the workout in the rain. My knees and muscles ached for weeks after. I was so committed and dedicated though that I exercised come rain or shine. It was so hot on one occasion that I developed blisters on the palms on my hands. And after completing 60 days, I'd start all over again, completing Insanity Asylum, Insanity T25 and, in more recent times, Insanity Max 30. New levels of super fitness saw me endure and build stamina to give limitless energy that fuelled my relentless and growing ambitions. But in spite of my growth and new-found self-determinism, I was still in a very dark place. My motivation wasn't born out of inspiration or love. Rather, it was anger and hatred towards a woman who had broken my heart and abandoned me. I wanted to do something so bold and outrageous that she'd get to hear about it on the other side of the world.

I would dream of her. In the dream, I enter a restaurant and find her sitting with friends. When she sees me, she freaks out in a hysterical rage, "What are you doing here? I don't want you in my life!"

As if a warning, it brought with it the moment I was dreading. Chloe appeared on my Facebook timeline, a picture with her new lover. My blood boiled. Even though we weren't friends on Facebook, we had plenty of mutual friends.

Enough likes and comments of congratulations, you guys are so cute together, ensured the Facebook algorithm would have me see it. Another jealous rage ensued, causing my neural network to short-circuit and unfriend everybody I had met through her, even giving some of my family members ultimatums to choose, her or me. Chloe went from being called "love" and "babe" to become known as "She-who-cannot-be-named".

More than harbouring any false hopes of us reuniting, I couldn't understand why she could move on with such ease, while I remained stuck. Why wasn't I healing? After many months of abstinence, I ventured back into the world of sex, as recommended by many as the best way to get over somebody. The experience was so repulsive that I almost threw up thereafter. The thought of sharing my body with somebody else disgusted me. A few more attempts just to make sure resulted in no satisfaction, apart from karma going full circle. I spent the night with a woman who confronted me after hearing about my mysterious ways from a friend, a previous conquest. The words hit hard like a hurricane: "You're good for the night, but you're not relationship material". I cared little for my reckless actions or the hurt I caused others until that point, so I decided to abstain and channel my sexual energy into business ventures.

Three years had passed since leaving the corporate world. I turned 33 years old and a friend remarked that I had entered my 'Jesus Year', the year that scholars believe Jesus of Nazareth was crucified in Jerusalem after starting a spiritual, political and intellectual revolution. The remark stayed with me into the coming weeks, growing louder in my thoughts. I had seen so much growth and progress by investing in my mental and physical well-being, but somehow I had reached a plateau – it was like running into a brick wall. And then, after decades of linking God exclusively with religion, I found God through spirituality. Instead of self-help and business books, I invested in books and went to seminars on spirituality. I was hooked. Some literature was strange, some profound and insightful. The more I discovered, the clearer everything became. It reminded me of growing up near-sighted and having a blurred picture until contact lenses changed my life – I could see and experience life in HD quality!

As I grew spiritually, so did my intuition. I became less interested in doing, and more relaxed on letting the dots connect themselves. Serendipity became

Chapter 8: That One Time I Stopped Time

as natural as breathing and I no longer pondered on "What are the odds!?" Asking the right questions became more important than knowing the answers, and the right people appeared at just the right time.

Life lesson: What you do is not as important as what you believe.

Time blurred like the casino floors in Las Vegas. Mondays, Fridays, weekends – it was all the same. Whether 1 am, 3 am, 8 am, 1 pm, 5 pm, 11 pm, it didn't matter. And on many occasions when looking at the time, it would be 11:11, 22:22 or 08:08, as if a sign or guidance from the universe that I was on the right track. Months of the year – January, June, only different by the season; December by when people took leave, leaving me waiting in frustration for decisions and actions that would only happen when they returned to work. My construct of time was being redefined, and it showed in my punctuality. I was always running late.

My beliefs about money changed too. When I left the corporate environment, I committed that the only money I'd ever earn would be through my own business ventures. And while I've never experimented with hard drugs, I could relate to coming off the addition called money. Before leaving HPS, I saved enough money to live off while trying to build a successful business, placing all my bets on the smart metering venture which didn't materialise. A steady flow of money left my bank account month after month. After three years with no income and my stubborn commitment to destroy the 'unhealthy middle class' mindset that defined my relationship with money, I was taking serious strain. At night I tossed and turned, waking up to cold sweats. "Give up" a voice in my head taunted, but I stood firm. And after some time, I would lie still as a corpse, staring dead into the ceiling, listening to the crickets' chirp and the clock tick "tick-tock-tick-tock your money is running out".

I was losing my mind. One night I woke up not knowing where I was. I sat up in bed feeling lost; everything looked unfamiliar. Panic set in when I couldn't recall my own name, then subsided a few moments later when my memory returned. On another occasion I woke up finding myself sitting upright, terrified, my ears zinging to a high-pitched frequency.

CHAPTER 9

LIVING ON THE EDGE OF CHAOS

Chapter 9
LIVING ON THE EDGE OF CHAOS

Another death on Facebook. It bothered me. When I die, I want them to delete my profile. "What happens to my Facebook account when I die?", but for once Google returned no answers apart from blogs by people who shared their experiences and suggestions on what to do. "How many dead user accounts and what was the growth rate of Facebook?", the Google searched revealed an article confirming around 30 million dead profiles at 8,000 deaths per day and 1 billion users. And what about the multitude of web services and applications like music and email that were popping up? What will happen to all these digital assets and online identities when people die?

Death had to take a back seat. My education venture was failing. It wasn't the technology; we were ten years ahead of our time. How could the Education Ministry or a school appreciate Single Sign-On and content aggregation services when they didn't even have decent connectivity, or had more pressing matters like infrastructure and facilities to invest in such as ablution facilities? I resolved to persist and stay committed, the opportunity and social impact far outweighed the wait and associated risks – besides, I had already lost out on a billion-rand opportunity, so failure wasn't as daunting. I continued to build a brand in basic education, exhibiting at an expo, visiting schools – both private and rural, and taking part in a leadership programme to help drive transformation. Visits to schools in Soweto brought back vague memories of my childhood; Soweto was still as vibrant as it was decades earlier. I also met with a senior official from the Education Ministry and the head of Corporate Social Investment (CSI) at a major private bank.

The Education Ministry was an interesting one. I had noted them as a strategic partner but made no contact, such was the reputation of any government department. Then one Sunday, out of desperation I sent them a message via the enquiry form on their website. Not expecting a reply, I received a response

Chapter 9: Living on the Edge of Chaos

first thing Monday morning, including the contact person who looked after partnerships. Later that morning, Louis e-mailed and was to the point. "We receive a huge number of requests, so please send me a proposal and if we like what you're saying we'll contact you." Fair enough I thought and sent him a business proposal. Before the week was over, Louis called. "We like your proposal; would it be possible for you to visit us at our offices in Pretoria?" Yes, I confirmed, containing my excitement. And then Louis asked, "Are you coloured?" Yes, I replied and asked why. "I can't tell from your accent, but I called to see who is this person from 'Rivaks' capable of putting this proposal together." Rivaks is slang for Riverlea, the 'coloured township' I've lived in all my life. Louis was the marketing director for the 2010 World Cup team and was based five minutes from my house at Soccer City, before taking on a post at the Education Ministry. He saw my home/office address on the cover page which prompted him to call. We met later that week to discuss a potential partnership and talk about our mixed heritage, where I learnt of his participation in our country's liberation struggle which saw him spend five years in prison. Before leaving his office, Louis added, You should consider forming a non-profit entity, that's our preference."

With SSO and content aggregation still ten years away, I pivoted the business model to focus on growing an online community for teachers. My American technology provider had a global teacher community they used as a marketing tool to get teachers to access their content and digital resources. I formed a South African group within the community and recruited teachers on my visits to schools. They always signed up, but never contributed any resources of their own. It puzzled me. How could we overcome this?

The leadership development programme to drive transformation in schools provided community building workshops which connected me with a lady named Thato. We were in the same group exercise and had to share our greatest fear. It was one of the rare occasions I allowed myself to be vulnerable in front of others and talk about the pain that had been consuming me. Thato found my story captivating and asked if her husband could call me. He had just resigned from the corporate environment to start his own business. Sure thing; there is a natural sense to give back once life has taught you some valuable lessons. I received a call later that night, "Hey Malcolm, it's me Sechaba, my wife gave me your number. We attended Sacred Heart College together…" I pretended to remember him but for the world couldn't. We agreed to meet. I checked my yearbooks after the call and as suspected, no Sechaba.

Family and friends had become accustomed to me obsessing and sharing ideas with them. My conversations were all over the place. It reached a point where they even put rules in place. Ten minutes and no more idea talks, or they'd talk about She-who-cannot-be-named. So I used my ten minutes to tell Mark about "death and social media", pointing out that we'd have a billion dead people online in a few generations. Once he got over the morbid nature of the topic, he agreed it was a good idea and asked, "What are you going to call it?" "I'm not sure, something to do with a vault, an online vault."

I held back the temptation to share details of other projects. In 2007, I had the privilege to attend an HPS training camp in Bristol in the UK, a trip that brought with it another visit to Anfield. My last visit was off season, so this time I got to see Liverpool FC play Manchester City live! I sat in the Paddock enclosure just three rows from the pitch and halfway between the team dugout and the famous Kop end. Steven Gerrard scored the only goal to see Liverpool victorious. It was priceless experience and reminded me about the time in church when I felt the presence of God. Maybe the concept of God was more about human connection and community than a traditional God? Home fixtures meant there was no accommodation in the city, so I had to share a room with a fellow South African. It was only for two days and the guy, much younger than me, seemed friendly enough. We retired early the night before the game to be up for the big day that lay ahead. In the early hours of the morning, I was woken up by this guy speaking in tongues in what sounded like Hebrew. "Excuse me?" I asked. His body remained still as he kept talking. Was he possessed? I have never been so terrified and didn't sleep a wink after. He awoke fresh while I was exhausted.

We travelled back to London by train and while staring out the window at the English countryside, an idea came to mind. We had grown up on English football, followed it religiously, but most of us never got to experience a live game, the pre-match build-up and post-match celebrations, nor the city. These thoughts gave birth to 'The Ultimate Fan Experience'. It would revolutionise the way sport clubs engaged with their global fan bases to create content that provided insights that many fans were unaware of. I returned home and drew up the business plans, even securing a copyright for the concept from the Library of Congress in the USA, registered under PAu003509779. The idea hasn't come into fruition, but it gave me confidence to dream at a global stage. I even reached out to Fenway Sports Group who acquired Liverpool FC in October 2010 and pitched the idea to one to their executives after finding him on LinkedIn. He replied, noting that the concept was interesting and that he'd forward it to management at the club. If they were interested, they'd contact me. I was ecstatic, even though no reply was forthcoming.

My love for sport and creating business opportunities led to another potential venture in Collegiate sports leagues, linking branding opportunities to their tailgating events on match day. College sports in the US is huge business. I engaged with manufacturers in China, worked with a business analyst from India and distribution companies in America, all from my living room table. Conversations were progressing with a distribution company based in Miami. Meetings were held via Skype and it came as a surprise to them to learn that I was based in South Africa. They withdrew interest, citing it was best if I had offices in the USA to de-risk the business. A Skype call with a manufacturer in China led to an awkward moment. There is a six-hour time difference, so a call was scheduled during their lunchtime. I was late as usual and had just a few minutes before the call. Skype calls are usually just audio, so I dialled in sitting in nothing but my underwear, only for the lady to activate the video feed. I dived out of sight and pretended the connection was bad, rebooting the router which bought me time to put on a shirt and freshen my face. Go Slow!

I then resolved to find opportunities closer to home and explored micro-financing, making a large loan to the owner of a small business that transported kids to and from school. The money went towards buying another vehicle. The idea was to provide finance and business support with the goal of launching a bus service that transported people from Johannesburg to Bulawayo in Zimbabwe. I visited the depot in Joburg CBD to confirm the demand for people travelling the planned route, noting that informal and un-banked sectors are an untapped goldmine. Repayments on the loan however were not forthcoming and ended my interest in both transportation ventures. Failure was fast becoming my best teacher.

I met Sechaba for coffee and it turned out he was a grade below me in primary school. Both of us left Sacred Heart College and lost touch for almost twenty years. It was refreshing to see him talk, his enthusiasm reminding me of when I started out three years prior. "You've got to come with me to this business breakfast get-together, it happens every other Thursday," he urged, as we went our separate ways. "Sure thing!", but many Thursday's would pass before taking him up on his invitation.

Life lesson: Opportunity waits for no one.

My signature move was sending out emails on a Sunday. The recipient would see it first thing Monday and think "Wow, this guy is dedicated". It was no different when I sent a mail to the head of the CSI division at a major private bank. He replied and agreed to meet. The meeting went well and he wanted to find a way for us to work together. Before ending the meeting, he set in motion a defining moment, "We prefer working with non-profit entities".

So on January 21st 2013, I founded a non-profit company and named it the Dr CL Smith Foundation as a tribute to the legacy of my late grandfather who had passed away five years earlier. It brought immense joy to come good on the commitment I had made at his funeral as his coffin passed through the doors at the crematorium and into the furnace. My grandmother teared up and then presented me with a box of old photos and documents. I used these artefacts as inspiration to write a dedication for the Foundation's website:

"Clifford Leon Smith was born 29 September 1928 in Johannesburg, South Africa to Maggie du Preez and Henry Gesant Jacobs. As a baby he suffered from polio and did not walk until he was four years old. As a young man he was a talented sprinter, played soccer, tennis and golf. He joined the Red Cross and was a keen scholar, accused of being lazy when he wanted to continue his education after completing Grade 10. His Red Cross membership inspired him to pursue a career as a medical doctor.

Chapter 9: Living on the Edge of Chaos

Through the sacrifice and efforts of his family, Clifford Leon Smith began his long and arduous journey in completing a Bachelor of Medicine and Surgery. Overcoming adversity under an apartheid government, he completed his first year at the University of Fort Hare before being allowed to transfer to the University of the Witwatersrand (Wits). During this time of enforced racial, social and economic segregation where laws defined a person's race, where they could live and spend their free time, how and where they could travel and work, and limited by a separate inferior system of education for Blacks—Clifford Leon Smith was the first coloured doctor to graduate at Wits University from the then Transvaal province. Dr Clifford Leon Smith later become the first non-white Assistant District Surgeon in Johannesburg.

Dr Smith dedicated his life to serving the healthcare needs of others and specialised as a Paediatrician, General Practitioner and District Surgeon.

In a career spanning 48 years, he worked at the Donald Fraser Hospital in Sibasa, Limpopo; Northdale Hospital in Pietermaritzburg, KwaZulu-Natal; various hospitals across Lesotho as the District Surgeon for the British High Commissioner; and the Chris Hani Baragwanath Hospital in Soweto before opening his own practice in Newclare, Johannesburg. Gifted in diagnosis and treatment, Dr Smith was also a compassionate doctor. He had strong interpersonal skills and took a special interest in the lives of his patients, empathetic to their plight under an apartheid government. He would later dedicate his life to the upliftment and development of the communities in which he served.

Dr Smith was first elected as a member of the South Western Management Committee of Johannesburg City Council on November 29th 1967 and served as the representative for Coronationville. He was re-elected to represent Ward 13 in 1969, 1971, 1984 and 1988 before serving as Chairman from November 1989 to March 1990. During his term in office he was an active and concerned Councillor who maintained a close relationship with the ratepayers in his ward, also serving on the Grants-in-Aid Committee. On September 29th 1994, the South Western Management Committee presented Dr Smith with a Testimonial to recognise the excellent service rendered by him to the residents of Johannesburg.

Dr Clifford Leon Smith succumbed to cancer on February 2nd 2008 and is survived by his wife Yvonne, 8 children, 23 grandchildren and 19 great-grandchildren.

When you speak to family, past patients and students, or colleagues of Dr Clifford Leon Smith, you hear about a rare combination of diagnostic genius, compassion and strength. His dedication to his family, patients and community was tireless and unequivocal. This personal strength of will is the legacy, and the ongoing aspiration of the Dr CL Smith Foundation."

Our first initiative under the non-profit venture stemmed from a local newspaper article that featured Kayle Wykes, a talented golfer from Riverlea who schooled at Sacred Heart College. I knew all about the talents of young Kayle, who is a great-grandchild to the late Dr Clifford Leon Smith. Our family spent Easter weekends at a resort on the Vaal River, and while the women relaxed by the poolside, the men played golf. Kayle joined us for his first round of golf at just 7 years of age. He was confident and cheeky, boasting about how he would reign victorious. Being 25 years his senior, I had no problem accepting his challenge. He stood no chance and I took great pleasure in defeating him. A rivalry was born. Fast forward two years and in May 2013, Kayle made his debut in world golf, representing South Africa at the European Championships that took place in Scotland. The European Championships is a World Junior Golf Scoreboard ranked event which saw Kayle compete at the highest level in his age group. He then earned a priority invitation to travel to Johor, Malaysia in December 2013 to compete in the Kids Golf World Championship and also qualified for the World Championship in the USA. Yet despite all Kayle's achievements, his greatest pleasure is beating me on the golf course. Competing at the highest level in any sport is an expensive business. After seeing so many talented sportsmen from our communities never reach their potential, I committed to give as much support as possible via our non-profit venture to ensure that Kayle has every chance of realising his dream to one day play on the PGA Tour. I created a Facebook page to keep people abreast of his progress and have hosted golf days with his parents to raise funds to help cover his travel expenses. There is nothing more satisfying than seeing Kayle develop and grow to represent his club,

Chapter 9: Living on the Edge of Chaos

province and country at only 12 years of age. No matter where his journey may lead, his influence and impact is already evident.

Never could I have predicted that a nine-year-old would be the reason for my first appearances on live TV news and radio interviews.

The year unfolded, as did the chaos. I struggled to articulate what I did for a living when people asked. After 4 years with no job or apparent income, family gossip entertained ideas that I had either won the lottery or was a member of the Illuminati.

A growing reputation as the 'go-to guy' connected me with a mobile telecommunications company who were interested in the work I was doing in schools. The meeting unfolded like an episode of Dragon's Den, leaving me defeated. These guys ripped into me and invalidated any achievement or idea put forward. I was way out of my league and they knew it. My energy levels were low in the days that followed until an email from Arthur: there was a tender out for mobile and data services. I called the dragons who scorched me days earlier, "I have an opportunity, are you guys interested?" A few months later, we won the tender and the dragons became friends. It represented two milestones. The first was another annuity income stream after property, and while the income was small, it has paid for my telecommunication and fuel bills. I then tried to replicate the annuity income model for schools by creating EduPay, a service that experimented with telecommunication and stationery products.

The 80/20 principle was in full effect; the smarter I worked, the more free time I had, even making me feel guilty for a while.

Coffee with Sechaba. It was great to reconnect with my friend after so many years, the freedoms that come with entrepreneurship evident as we'd meet up and spend hours chatting about business and life during the 9 to 5 work week. He was an avid reader and spoke about a book he had read on quantum physics. It was a conversation that forever changed the way I understood life, revealing secrets unknown. Sechaba explained, "The book doesn't focus on the mechanics of quantum physics, but more about how one could use its paradigms to manifest reality." I wasn't buying it. The one part that grabbed my attention though related to why we never find happiness. "We're never happy because we link our happiness to some future event that may or may not happen." He had a point. I had perfected the art of "I'll be happy when…" conversations. Never content, never satisfied, never celebrating any accomplishment. And before going our separate ways, Sechaba reminded me, "Hey, when are you joining me for this breakfast meeting, there is one this Thursday". Sure thing, I promised to attend.I purchased the book on quantum physics, titled 'Why quantum physicists never fail' by Greg Kuhn. The book didn't use complex scientific jargon, but instead related to life and why we thought and acted the way we did. The analogies and insights were brilliant as Greg set the scene of what a pre-scientific world looked like; how the classic science revolution influenced our thinking and the resulting applications across various fields and disciplines like economics, medicine, engineering, government, biology and religion; how this Newtonian thinking then influenced great writers, statesmen and thinkers like Adam Smith, Sigmund Freud, Thomas Jefferson, Frederick Taylor, Karl Marx and Charles Darwin. Freud used the paradigm of determinism to create a new disciple of psychotherapy, and in the process inspired Darwin to create evolutionary biology. Greg then reveals the second scientific revolution that is underway, delving into the microscopic (subatomic) particles and macroscopic (immense) bodies in our universe – quantum physics. Could this be the invisible and mysterious force of God? From a paradigm perspective, it spoke to WHY we do the things the way we do them, and then compared classic science to quantum physics paradigms, a revelation that altered the neural pathways in my brain to forever change the way I perceived the world. It was a ghostly moment as I read through and comprehended the various paradigms of Mechanism versus Holism, Determinism versus Unity, Separateness versus Entanglement and Logical Outcomes versus Nonlinearity. I became overwhelmed, feeling like I had been asleep for 33 years.

The book revealed the most painful life lesson: Our neural pathways of habitual thought form our beliefs, our beliefs set our expectations, and our expectations manifest our reality in a physical realm of infinite possibilities. We are responsible for all our life's experiences, including suffering.

Thursday morning arrived and I was determined to come good on my promise to join Sechaba at the business breakfast session. I had fallen victim to the 'snooze' pandemic and hold the world record of snoozing for two hours at 10-minute intervals. Despite efforts to get there early, I arrived 30 minutes late crawling in morning traffic. For years I avoided all forms of traffic, so it was a shock to my system to sit in bumper-to-bumper traffic at 6:30 am. How are people able do this every morning and afternoon, five days a week? I walked into the boardroom 20-minutes late to looks of 'who is this guy', only for Sechaba to rescue me. I sat and listened and didn't understand a word that was being said. "Admin scales, tone levels, PTS", they may as well have been talking a foreign language, which made me reminisce about my travels to Romania where I didn't understand what they were saying either. At breakfast, I met Simon, an elderly man, very humble and unassuming. You're likely to miss that he is a billionaire who made his fortune off property. Later that morning, we visited their Learning Academy where Sechaba had attended several courses. I met Stacey who ran the centre. In her office hung certificates with all her achievements at the institution. "Doh!" Homer Simpson's voice shouted in my mind, "How did I land up here at this cult!?" Stacey explained what they offered in terms of personal and professional development, and I countered by expressing my views on organised religion, albeit a modern one. She acknowledged my concerns and the reputation their church had had, assuring me it wasn't the case. I agreed to the assessment. The results showed that I was strong and confident in my abilities, and then Stacey exposed the pain behind the brave face I was masking, "Despite all the positive things happening in your life, you remain unhappy". Homer's voice taunted me again – "Doh!" She saw right through me. "Ok, I am open to learn more, but let's keep it on the business track, and no taking part in the church stuff." She chuckled and agreed. Before leaving her office, I enquired what she did outside the centre. "Oh, I help the family with our commercial development interests. We own shopping malls, game lodges and residential developments." "So, you know the old man who hosts the breakfast sessions?" "Yes, he's my father." I often struggle to deduce the simple things in life. Go Slow!

Within a year of our chat, their family broke away from the church after a fallout with its leadership, who expelled them for refusing to abide by the rules. Expulsion meant disconnection, and disconnection meant members had to disown family and friends who criticised or disobeyed the church. My conclusion: there is no religion that can save me.

2013 saw entrepreneurship drift into the mainstream and I attended a three-day Start-up event which showed budding entrepreneurs how to go from ideation to launching a commercial product. A group of 30 attended, all males. Participants had 10 minutes to pitch their ideas, followed by a vote, and then groups formed around those with the most votes. I pitched the 'Death and Social Media' concept, an online vault that manages online properties in the inevitable event of one's death. It was a Friday night and the room fell quiet and uncomfortable as I shared the idea. Grappling with their mortality was too much to digest and my pitch received no votes.

Having multiple ventures on the go felt like having triplet babies all fighting for my attention. I struggled to choose, struggled to let go. I was like a single dad trying to raise three infants. And despite all the adversity, each child brought joy into my life. They grew up quick, each developing traits and personalities of their own.

I attended the Making CSI Matter 2013 Conference and met Charlotte, principal of a low-cost independent school in Yeoville. Once one of the 'trendiest' places in Johannesburg, today it's a receptive sponge for the downtrodden. Pinetree High School (PHS) was an oasis in a desert and had been around for 23 years under the guidance and leadership of Charlotte. We hit it off and made plans to meet. I visited the school a week later, impressed by what was possible, no matter the location or financial means.

Simon agreed to mentor Sechaba and myself. He turned 70 years old and in spite of accumulating a fortune, explained that it wouldn't be worth anything if he didn't give back by nurturing future leaders and pioneers. After reading Rich Dad Poor Dad all those years ago, I had finally found my rich dad. It was nothing like I imagined. Expecting to get insider secrets and a formula to the get-rich sauce, Simon was instead an attentive listener and spent the majority of our sessions letting us do the talking, only to pause and say, "Wow, you guys are so much farther than I was when I was your age". And when we complained about the struggles and elusiveness of that tipping point rags-to-riches moment, he reassured us it was just a matter of time, and to enjoy the struggle. "The pleasure and greatest reward is in the overcoming of the struggle." Sechaba and I listened on in disbelief and later joked, "He surely must be holding out on the secret sauce". But upon hearing Simon's incredible journey from living in the wilderness for five years to losing everything, and then building a family fortune over 30 year period starting at 40 years of age, he was right. An ever-diminishing bank balance and slow progress on ventures didn't keep me out of sleep anymore. Instead, I marvelled at the achievement and embraced the struggle. I had survived four years with no income, was debt free and about to vacation in Thailand for 12 days.

We spent four days in Bangkok and seven days in Phuket for a memorable vacation. Our travel party, a group of 10 people, made up of family and their spouses or significant others. In Bangkok, we were up early and on the road by 9 am to spend the day sightseeing and shopping, followed by afternoon massages, and at night we'd roam the city and party until 5 am. Bangkok is the New York of the East. And while everybody in the group was in a relationship, I was single and free to experience everything that Thailand had to offer. The others lived vicariously through me as I returned to share tales of adventure, conquest and soapy massages. In Phuket, we soaked up the sun and took day trips to all the famous islands. On day 7, I fell ill with nausea at breakfast. The last time I had fallen ill was two years ago when She-who-cannot-be-named abandoned me. The group went down to Phuket Beach and I remained in the hotel room, sleeping into the afternoon to wake up feeling much better, and deciding not to join the rest of the group. The 'Overcoming work and life stress' course I was on started to resonate. It introduced the notion of suppressive elements, whether circumstances or people, which result in mistakes or illness if not dealt with; and PTS, whereby a suppressed person becomes a Potential Trouble Source to themselves. It was all making sense. There were aggressive and antisocial people in our group, which elevated my stress levels leading to illness. I acknowledged this as the reason for my illness and confronted it as opposed to the heat, food or other unknown reasons earlier deduced. That acknowledgement alone made me feel better. Another childhood belief dispelled: "Don't play in the rain children, you'll catch a cold". It's not the rain or cold that makes a child ill, rather it's the nagging parent that stresses the child, making their immune system vulnerable, that leads to illness. When reuniting with the group, I found two more members had fallen ill with stomach bugs. They opted to stay with the group and suffered with illness for two days. I thought about telling the group about the revelation, but knew they'd think I was crazy – even I thought I was crazy. I needed to finish this course once I got back home. The drama continued upon returning home from Thailand. An argument ensued over money owed for alcohol. I argued to being subjected to unfair treatment as my contribution was the same amount as the couples, even though I was single. The argument persisted into the coming days, at which point I mentioned to my Insanity Workout partner, "It wouldn't surprise me if something happens to her", explaining what I had learnt about suppressive people and PTS. The next day her appendix burst and brought with it the revelation: I knew why I no longer fell ill. I had removed all the suppressive people and elements in my life, and when I felt a cold coming on, I looked for the source of suppression and

confronted it. I thought back to school about the kid who carried the Bible and prayed and didn't fall ill. Was there a connection?

Phone call, 'Private Number'. I hate these anonymous calls, but answered. "Hi Mr Mooi, it's your financial planner, can I chat to you about some investment products?" I declined; doesn't this fool know I'm near broke. And just as the thought left my mind, a light bulb moment occurred, signalling two weeks of no sleep as my brain operated at capacity for my mind to architect a new path for the online vault venture. I encountered much resistance when talking about death and social media, so the financial planner ignited a spark that connected dots to pivot from digital legacy to financial wellbeing. Past events that lay dormant, deep in my memory recesses were now alive and the basis to unlock creativity and innovation.

Memory 1: When working at HPS and earning a decent income, it occurred to me I didn't have a Last Will and Testament. While I had no dependents, it still bothered me. So I visited my bank and applied for a Will. After completing the form, the lady explained the choice of storing it in their vault at an annual fee, or take it home to store in a safe place, but not before warning that most times Wills were so well hidden that they often weren't found when somebody died. "I'll take my chances," smirking as I left her office, "These banks sure know how to suck you dry!"

Memory 2: After leaving corporate and watching my bank balance diminish month after month, I had to cede a retirement annuity policy. The financial planner who sold it to me had long left the company, and the company had been acquired by another insurance company. Ceding meant waiting until 2035 for the policy to mature before being paid out.

Memory 3: Earning sales commissions are awesome when landing a big deal. The risks are high, but the rewards are worth it. I'm still living off the commission I made back in 2009. It was during this time I interacted with a financial planner on how to invest my money. The forms were so exhausting that we never got around to completing a financial needs analysis.

Google changed the way we accessed and qualified information. It's my #1 tool for architecting ideas and scheming business ventures. Search results pointed to unclaimed benefits. Research revealed that there are three million South Africans owed R45 billion in unclaimed pension fund benefits. This scenario is common to countries across the globe. The scale of unclaimed long- and short-term insurance and investment products in South Africa runs into the billions annually. The Financial Services Board states that there are many reasons billions of rands are still unclaimed, including the failure of employers and funds to provide information about beneficiaries, poor administration, the many foreign workers who leave the country soon after their work permits expire, failure of members to inform their dependants that they can claim benefits on their death, and outdated or well-hidden Wills. Measures to resolve this challenge have been reactive and limited to tracer companies, searchable databases and campaigns. It seemed very convenient for financial institutions to make money off us, then when they had to pay out, there were many reasons they didn't. It's a matter of banking ethics. On the estate planning side, I learnt that many people do not have their affairs in order which delays wrapping up an estate and also exposes people to generational wealth loss. Furthermore, we lose up to a third of our net wealth to fees and costs when transferring assets.

All these factors led me to create an online asset registry and planning tool that would provide people with peace of mind in these times of need. The goal was to empower and educate people to organize, securely store and share all their important personal, financial, legal and health information, all in one convenient place. The service would create better connections between people and key stakeholders like banks, insurance houses, financial and estate planners, intermediaries and law firms so loved ones weren't burdened or affected by the associated tribulations of death. And once this was all formulated, the online vault needed a name. I opted for mydigivault.net and registered the domain on September 2nd, 2013. The only thing more difficult than drawing up a complex business proposal is coming up with a domain name that is still available!

Thailand exposed me to custom-fitted clothing and birthed another business venture. Going way over budget, I purchased two suits, six shirts, three pants and a jacket which was still cheaper than what it would cost in SA. Instead of flying to Thailand, I explored 3D scanners to take exact measurements for the tailors, which once completed, were shipped directly to clients. Sechaba was fast becoming a networking guru and connected me with other entrepreneurs who had similar interests in the world of men's fashion. It made sense to work as a team, instead of individuals. The collaboration connected me with Alex, who later became a co-founder of MyDigiVault.

More 'children' meant more mouths to feed, bums to clothe and more problems to solve. At least I didn't have to raise this child on my own.

After many visits to Yeoville and chats with Charlotte, I had uncovered an opportunity to create value at Pinetree High School (PHS). My mission was to either reduce costs or create new revenue streams. PHS had used a leader in the retail space to purchase all their stationery. Could we source it cheaper without compromising on the quality? I reached out to a local manufacturer of stationery. The owner subjected me to Dragon's Den treatment, but it didn't faze me this time as we worked towards a comparative quote. We came in R65,000 cheaper than the leading retailer, even after my commission payment, which I had negotiated with the supplier as a rebate. I needed to earn a living, but not at the direct expense of school. Charlotte later told me they used the savings to take the kids to the Civic Theatre, a first for many of the kids. 2014 maintained

Chapter 9: Living on the Edge of Chaos

a blistering pace as life continued to test my resilience in the unknown and unfamiliar; it was a time of self-discovery. I completed a Personality Test on 16personalities.com which was based on the Myers-Briggs Indicator. It revealed a freakishly accurate description of who I was and even alluded to why I did things the way I did. INTJ – Introverted, Intuitive, Thinker, Judgmental. INTJs are 'Architects' or 'Masterminds' and form just 2% of the population. "It is often a challenge for them to find like-minded individuals to keep up with their relentless intellectualism and chess-like manoeuvring. Many INTJs are likely to have difficulties dealing with anything that does not need logical reasoning, and this weakness is visible in interpersonal relationships. INTJs find it very difficult to handle romantic relationships in their early stages." Knowing this brought me some peace but didn't subdue the extreme loneliness I had been suffering from. Could my personality be changed to improve interpersonal relationships? It bothered me for weeks on end. I craved to love and be loved, yet my personality stood in the way. "Rules, limitations and traditions are an anathema to the INTJ personality—they are bent on deconstructing and rebuilding every idea and system they come into contact with, using a sense of perfectionism and even morality to this work." Were my religious views and rebellion just down to my personality? Despite the freakishly accurate revelation, I hated labels and hated being put into a box, so I dug deeper to see if there was more to it. Another revelation followed based on three insights: 1) There are things we know we know. 2) There are things we know we don't know, and 3) There are things we don't know we don't know. Numbers 1 and 2 are introspection, easy to reflect on and talk about. Number 3 is difficult as there are no answers, no absolutes, only questions – was I asking the right questions? Attempting to discover what you don't know you don't know is a painful yet liberating experience. It's an attempt at understanding the construction of thought and behaviours. Yes, my personality influenced my behaviour and actions, but it wasn't who I was. Who I am, was more about my awareness and how I perceived myself and others.

I would dream about her. Walking into a bedroom, I'd see them sleeping in a warm embrace. It felt peaceful. She was happy. I was happy for her, if only in the dream, for I'd wake up to feelings of hatred towards She-who-cannot-be-named.

The previous year introduced me to quantum physics and Scientology; this new year exposed me to Hermetic teachings, astral projection and the work of Joseph Campbell.

My mom and I attended a 'Find you inner Genius' seminar. The two-day seminar introduced us to A Hero's Journey, the blueprint for many Hollywood blockbusters including the Matrix, Lord of the Rings and Star Wars. It was fascinating and mapped like a blueprint onto my own life's journey, the struggles, demons and serendipitous moments. They weren't random anymore. The seminar also touched on some texts in the Hermetic corpus, which our facilitator mentioned dated back to the 6th century BC in ancient Egypt and Greece. Day One ended with a meditation. Before we left, delegates shared what they had experienced. On the drive home, my mother shared her experience. It was the same as mine, which was strange as everybody else had different experiences, the open spaces of our visions perhaps a sign of the spiritual journey we were on. Our relationship had evolved from parent-child to friendship. My mom had joined our non-profit venture and was working on an Early Childhood Development project. She also joined me for the Insanity Workouts, which was impressive at her age. Many have come and gone, Insanity getting the better of them, but my mom has kept at it.

The Kybalion by the Three Initiates guided me through hermetic philosophy. While complex to read, cryptic and abstract, it was insightful for ascertaining an ancient civilisation's understanding of how the universe worked. The principles of Mentalism, Correspondence, Vibration, Polarity, Rhythm, Cause & Effect and Gender were profound. I noticed a common thread between this and the work of Joseph Campbell – the mythologist best known for his work in comparative mythology and comparative religion, and Alan Watts – the British philosopher, writer and speaker, best known as an interpreter and populariser of Eastern philosophy for a Western audience. The most startling revelation was the Principle of Polarity. It shook me the same way as being exposed to quantum physics paradigms and learning that I was passive aggressive; moments when the unconscious became conscious. Polarity embodies the truth that all manifested things have 'two sides'; 'two aspects'; 'two poles', only separated by degrees. Anything in the physical realm needed its polar opposite to exist. For example, hot and cold are the same, only differing in degrees of temperature. East and west are the same, only differing in degrees of direction. Love and hate are the same, only differing in degrees of emotion. Boom! It hit me like a hammer over the head. I still had feelings for She-who-cannot-be-named. And like the alchemist who turned silver into gold, I turned my feelings of hatred into love – love that was free from expectation. It brought me peace.

I would dream of her. This time I found myself in an apartment where Chloe and her lover were laying on a couch, laughing as they watched TV. I felt the mood change seeing her move to the opposite end of the room while he remained on the couch. He was still laughing, but she was annoyed.

With my awareness level at an all-time high, I experienced astral projection or what is known as an out of body experience. It ranks as my most significant life event that is still vivid in my mind. I was lying in bed on my back drifting off to sleep when I sat up. Sitting up felt strange in that I was semi-conscious and knew my 'physical body' remained lying down. I stood up by the edge of my bed, my 'eyes' still closed, and sensed everything around me, objects and spaces. Panic set in as thoughts rushed into and flooded my mind. What's happening, where do I go, what if I can't find my way back to my body? The thoughts then grew silent. The more I relaxed, the more I could sense things around me, things beyond my bedroom, our house, our neighbourhood, beyond our city. I experienced emotions that ranged from enlightenment to peace, to joy, to love, to reason, to acceptance, until I stopped judging the experience and feelings to find myself become one with the universe. It was like I had tapped into infinite knowledge and in this absence of thought, I came to fully experience God. As my awareness grew, I could feel a tingling sensation rush over my physical body. It was as if you placed beads on a subwoofer speaker and turned the volume up to a max, leaving the beads to levitate on the sound waves. I tried to rationalise what had happened, thinking about what I had learnt in quantum physics about particles and waves, or the Principle of Vibration in Hermetic teachings, but it was beyond my comprehension. I bought a book on astral projection to gain a better understanding hoping I could experience it again, but it has eluded me ever since.

Just past the midpoint of 2014, Privest Bank approved funding for my venture in education. Two years had passed since I proposed the concept of an online community for teachers after observing that there was no culture of sharing and collaboration in the sector. Zibuza is isiZulu for 'we ask' and relates to developing one's intellect. Our social networking community for South African teachers was finally going to be built and I would finally get to make use of the domain name, zibuza.net, which I had registered on December 21st, 2011. This significant milestone came with mixed emotions. We had asked for R900,000 for a 12-month proof-of-concept, with Privest Bank only prepared to commit R500,000. I negotiated the suppliers down to R550,000 which secured us the funding, but it meant I had to remove any money that would pay me a salary; my calm and collected reaction perhaps a sign of my growth, perhaps of my mental instability. Either way, I was at an all-time low. Once the money reached our bank account, I questioned how much I had given of myself – the savings, pension and investments that I had cashed in all surfaced. My personal bank balance was depleted, but the business account reflected a small fortune. I resolved it best to pay our suppliers before temptation set in.

With the funding secured for zibuza.net, I decided to withdraw from the men's fashion venture as I had way too much on my plate. Alex and I had developed a great rapport, so I invited him to co-found MyDigiVault, registering a company on August 29th, 2014. The Fintech space was booming, and we needed to make a move if we wanted to capitalise on the opportunity to disrupt the financial sector.

As far as Christmas gifts go, this year I received news at a family get together that Chloe had gotten married. Like the time I matriculaed from school and had to make peace with not going back to Sacred Heart College, the news brought with it the ultimate closure.

Development of zibuza.net began in September and kept me occupied until February. I was leading two companies to build and integrate platforms, one American, the other South African. The end product was a social networking platform, enabling teachers to engage and interact with one another, while an incentive platform tracked all the social interactions which we used to reward teachers for their participation and contributions. It was a global effort. The CEO of the American company was based in London, with the project management team based in Alameda, California, and their development team split across Russia and the Ukraine. Countless Skype calls later saw me reading emails in a Russian/Ukrainian accent. It was interesting to note that while we worked together as a multinational team, mainstream news blasted coverage of the conflict between Russia and the Ukraine.

Privest Bank also afforded me the opportunity to take part in a leadership development programme for non-profit companies. It was great to engage with like-minded individuals and work with life coaches. The group met once a month, and with our life coaches as often as needed. My life coach was a qualified psychologist, and instead of following the coursework, our sessions deviated with me pouring my heart out. I had been harbouring and suppressing emotions for so long, I had become robot-like. Our sessions gave me an outlet to share my grief and emotions with somebody who listened without judgement or advice. It was just the therapy I needed and the impact was evident in the presentations made at the final group session. People noted the growth in my development over the six months, my vulnerability exposing a sensitive and compassionate person behind the one-dimensional machine. The programme closed with the group sitting in a half-moon arrangement, each person having time to sit in the middle while other members appreciated them. It was an emotional experience that had many people fighting to hold back their tears, myself included. A tribute from a lady praising my character and courage concluded with words that brought the tears, "I have a young son and I hope that he grows up to be someone like you". A compliment that touched my soul; the validation somewhat peculiar in that the lady was white. While I thought I had long disposed of my race filter, childhood memories that formed core beliefs of inferiority still lingered in my mind, even though this lady saw me as a person and not for the colour of my skin or the associated stereotypes. If you remove privilege, perhaps white people are just as much victims of apartheid and racism as people of colour. We are all robbed of opportunity.

Curiosity haunted me as I wondered why Facebook had not exposed me to Chloe's wedding photos. What did she look like on her big day? I committed not to stalk her profile, so asked Arthur if he had heard anything, knowing they kept in touch. His reply was somewhat surprising, "Dude, she broke up with the guy two months ago". Strange, that was around the time I had the dream and sensed all was not well. My spiritual journey revealed that even though we did not share a connection in the physical realm anymore, we were still connected in the spiritual realm through a soul tie. A Christian friend confirmed that even the Bible speaks about it, referencing Matthew 19:5, 1 Samuel 18:1 and Genesis 34:2-3. And while I still struggled to understand the scriptures in the Bible, the text likened to legal jargon, I learnt to appreciate the common values thanks to the insights provided by Joseph Campbell on comparative religions. We were just using different languages to express our relationship with God. While many years my senior, Charlotte and I had become great friends. At one of our catch-up-over-coffee sessions, she shared news of reuniting with an old love interest that went back some 30 years. The hopeless romantic in me saw a great love story with a happy ending, the impulsive teenager in me didn't want to wait 30 years, so after 4 years of no communication, I contacted Chloe, sending her an email describing the day I dropped her off at the airport, and then invited her to entertain an alternate ending to our story where I didn't sabotage our friendship.

She replied after a week telling me I didn't live in reality, that we weren't friends and she would never ever trust me, ending the mail with a request to never contact her again.

CHAPTER 10

WHY CAN WE REMEMBER THE PAST, BUT NOT THE FUTURE?

Chapter 10
WHY CAN WE REMEMBER THE PAST, BUT NOT THE FUTURE?

We launched zibuza.net on March 1st 2015, and as teachers signed up, I noted every aspect of their experience. Aware of my OCD tendencies, I held back on coercing them to make the most of the community. The proof-of-concept made for 12 months of hard lessons learnt, the silver lining hidden in these same lessons adding to my personal growth and changing my perspective on failure.

I stopped telling myself sad stories and came to view failure as a pathway to success, adopting a **"fail fast, fail often, fail forward"** attitude.

In the same month of launching zibuza.net, we received news that MyDigiVault had qualified as a semi-finalist in the SWIFT Innotribe Global Challenge. Over 500 judges from across the world, representing financial, technology and investment communities evaluated 370 applications, assessing a start-ups' ability to provide an important innovation in the financial industry. MyDigiVault was among the TOP 8 early stage start-up companies to take part in the first ever African semi-final showcase taking place in Cape Town on May 6th, 2015.

Tensions mounted between Alex and myself, and we argued like husband and wife. His spouse coincidentally grew up in Riverlea. Two years my senior, their generation were the cool kids, and just hanging out with them validated our coolness. Like so many people I've reacquainted with over time, it came as no surprise when Alex introduced his wife.

While all failures lead to success, some failures are harder than others to process and accept. Our zibuza.net community was growing at a slow pace. People signed up but weren't signing in, and many weren't taking part or making contributions. It puzzled me. This time we had a pot of R50,000 to give teachers for their participation and contributions. I thought the lure of money would be the carrot on the stick that got the donkey moving. The data showed it wasn't. My financial situation worsened and pressure mounted, though Privest Bank added R40,000 to the project's budget to ease my suffering. The rewards company also paid R10,000 in commission for the business I had brought them. I had survived 6 years with no salary, reinvesting every cent earned back into the businesses. The money was like a gasp of oxygen after holding my breath for too long. Living a minimalistic lifestyle, I could stretch R50,000 to at least 12 months. While most people earned money to keep up with their lifestyle, the money I earned bought time.

When the time was up, the dream was up.

Despite zibuza.net still being in a proof-of-concept stage, the platform qualified as a semi-finalist in the GAP ICT innovation challenge. The competition called on innovators and entrepreneurs in Gauteng Province to propose novel business concepts based around ICTs that would improve people's lives and enhance service delivery by government. Perhaps much-needed validation that we were on the right track.

Project reviews with Privest Bank happened every few months. A visit to their offices demanded wearing a suit, a stark contrast to my home office where the typical attire was just underwear or a track pants and t-shirt. Their offices are in Sandton, Africa's richest square mile along with the most important business and financial districts. The meeting got underway and I led in disclosing the challenges we were facing, including the action plans to turn things around. They were ever supportive, offering advice which gave me comfort to alert them about the challenge I couldn't resolve. Our rewards' supplier had issued a VAT exclusive invoice for our project that was all inclusive. It threw the budget out by R57,000. "Why would I overshoot the budget by R57,000 after removing all my earnings to get the deal done?" I tried to reason with the rewards supplier, but they weren't willing to compromise; they claimed to have already paid the VAT to SARS. Was it miscommunication on my part? Short-sightedness and greed on their side? It was a mess. The meeting ended to parting words of, "Tell them we won't be releasing any more funds". The VAT dispute took my attention off the project and escalated into a feud that saw me win the battle, but lose the war.

MyDigiVault was a member of Microsoft's BizSpark programme that supported entrepreneurs. With our qualification in the Innotribe Challenge, BizSpark offered to pay for our flights, accommodation and car rental to spend the week in Cape Town. I had long forgotten about corporate travel, so I felt like a professional athlete getting sponsored to compete at an international sporting event.

I flew to Cape Town a few days earlier to spend time with my best friend Sebastian, his lovely wife Jaclyn and their two beautiful daughters, Hannah and Amy. It was a timeless friendship. We met at Sacred Heart College and remained close friends even after I had left, staying close into adulthood, before he moved to further his studies. It was interesting to observe family life and I couldn't help but ponder what I was missing out on. My life appeared to be glamorous and exciting, always on the go, but it was lonely for the most part and deep down I craved to have the family they were building. It was a rude awakening though having to wake up 5 am every morning to the cries and playfulness of the girls as they woke with unlimited amounts of energy and complexity to get their needs met.

The Innotribe experience was world class. We had two days of training before the big event. It was much needed too as my practice pitch exposed I had no clue what to do. We had 6 minutes to pitch; I took 10+ minutes. My presentation was so poor, the coaches enquired if I was trying to save the world. Late nights and early mornings with guidance from mentors saw us polish the presentation to perfection. Once back at the hotel room, I'd lie in bed and run through the presentation, over and over, even recording and listening to it on repeat as I fell asleep. The big day flew by as fast as the six minutes that contestants had to pitch. Early indications had us among the favourites to go through to the finals, which was happening in Singapore in November. It was nerve-wracking to wait for the announcement, networking with the organisers and delegates our only distraction. MyDigiVault didn't make it through, we were the only semi-finalist who didn't have a working prototype or any traction. The disappointment was short-lived as we unwound on post conference cocktails, a gala dinner and an evening of entertainment and the V&A Waterfront. It was an unforgettable experience and despite not making it through, we received interest from a major consulting firm, who later introduced us to a major bank.

All three companies who made it were alumni of a local accelerator programme run by a husband and wife duo. I had to get us into their accelerator and so I did.

Back to Johannesburg and the ongoing VAT dispute with our rewards supplier. Zibuza.net user engagement was increasing. The community was attracting professionals like education psychologists, behavioural practitioners, motivational speakers and occupational therapists. While most programmes in education focused on curriculum content, we were focusing on holistic skills. It made me think about the difficult times I experienced when changing schools. How was I supposed to learn and do well when neither myself, parents or teachers knew how to handle the emotional trauma I was experiencing?

Tensions between Alex and I grew to sleepless nights and eczema breakouts. My insensitive INTJ nature was exposed when Alex couldn't attend a meeting with software developers because of a family emergency: his father-in-law rushed to hospital for a suspected heart attack. My reply, "Can the meeting go ahead without you?" It reached breaking point when we were accepted into the accelerator programme and Alex withdrew his participation, objecting to the homework' and R5,000 investment. This, from one of the hardest working guys I knew. It was time to serve divorce papers, a tough decision and awkward moment that again had the exact opposite outcome of expected unpleasantries. Alex and I had different ways of working which was causing us to clash. Also, it was another example of pursuing and building your dream versus helping somebody else build theirs. When Alex joined me on MyDigiVault, he put his own business venture on hold.

Like Arthur, we remain close friends and meet every Sunday for a morning run, discussing the progress on our ventures and the many trials and tribulations that entrepreneurship has to offer.

While both business ventures are data driven, the real interest was human behaviour. Why do we think and act as we do, and how can behaviour be modified? It fascinated me and became an obsession. It was interesting to learn more about the brain and how we develop skills to achieve mastery. More interesting was the primitive (instinct) and analytic (logic) nature of the brain. Take my fear of birds: all it took was one crow to chase and terrorise me, causing me to freak out whenever a bird is close by. The logical part of my brain says birds are not out to harm me, my primitive brain recalls the crow that terrorised me and overrides everything to go into survival mode. Another example was associating memories with places, like all the places Chloe and I had frequented. My logical brain said those are your favourite restaurants, my primitive brain said don't go back there as your heart will be broken. If our past influences our current reality in the way our mind stores and processes memories, then perhaps we could reprogram our brains to stop reacting to our past experiences? I turned to some of my spiritually enlightened friends. They confirmed what I had read up on and then some, sharing knowledge on how to find the 'bad' memory, confront it and remove the power it had on one's behaviour. They called it 'going clear'. Then things got weird, as it turns out our memories are not just from this lifetime but from past lives too, as they shared stories about a lady who couldn't conceive until discovering and confronting that she had died in a miscarriage in her previous life, and of a friendship where one friend had power over another, only to discover it was a pact they had made in a previous life in an era of war where they both died in combat. Doubt and judgement are natural reactions, but imagine memories over several lifetimes and how our primitive minds are using these bad experiences to influence our current behaviour and actions?

Time is a great healer of wounds, and I was ready to start dating again. Hello Tinder. The online dating application that uses your location and Facebook information to create a profile made up of your first name, age, Facebook photos and any pages you've liked, to show common interests with potential matches. You find prospective matches near you by sexual preference, age and distance. If you fancy, swipe right to 'like' them, otherwise go left to 'pass'. If they swipe right – bingo, it's a match and you can message. Perfect for introverts. Dating was like learning to ride a bike again and I needed training wheels after being out of the dating game and social scenes for so long. It followed a pattern: conversations progressed from Tinder, to Whatsapp, to a date. The more I swiped, the more dates I went on, the more my confidence grew, but not without signature awkward moments. One date went well, or

Chapter 10: Why can we Remember the Past, but not the Future?

so I thought. The conversation was great, the chemistry was evident, and when the bill came, we split it 50/50. I thought about gender equality and how attractive independent women were, but she ignored me thereafter and then said she didn't think I was into her when not offering to pay the bill. It puzzled me – where is the logic? I met Charlotte for dinner and explained how events had unfolded, only for her to laugh at my aloofness, suggesting I practice with her. It was all about the timing she said. So later, when Charlotte reached for her handbag, I reached for her hand and said, "Don't worry, I'll get this one", only for her to reply, "I'm just getting a tissue". Go Slow!

Tinder was reminiscent of my 20s, but with a digital spin to adventure and conquest, with predators on both sides.

One such conquest took an interesting turn to the bedroom. Swipe right. Match. Message. Whatsapp. Let's meet up. At dinner, the conversation and red wine flowed. After a few laughs, she invited me back to her place on one condition, "no funny business". I agreed and followed her home. We spent the evening conversing about life and compared battle scars. She took a real interest when I spoke about quantum physics. "Our neural pathways of habitual thought form our beliefs, our beliefs set our expectations, and our expectations manifest our reality in a physical realm of infinite possibilities," I explained and added, "That's why it's possible to remember the future." She seemed perplexed and asked for an example, so I explained that we remembered the past as a collapsed space-time event, and that we struggle to remember the future because our brains cannot process the infinite data streams of future time-space possibilities. To remember and manifest the future, we had to set forth our expectations and focus our attention on collapsing time-space to match our grandest desires and truest beliefs. The trick is in truly believing; the quantum field isn't fooled by surface-level desires. So in our instance, there was an infinite amount of future realities of "no funny business", but also an infinite amount of future realities that would see us move the conversation to the bedroom. It all depended on our truest beliefs and grandest desires. "So what future are you remembering now?" she smirked. "I believe the one where we collapse time-space for some funny business," taking her hand as we made our way to her bedroom.

The same truest belief and grandest desire rules of quantum physics that got me laid, connected me with Zoe. While the dating scene was fun and swiping addictive, I longed for connection and depth. If you translate quantum physics into prayer it would read, "Please God, I know there is someone out there for me. If you put her on my path, I promise to show up and be fully present. Amen." God chose Tinder, but hey, who am I to judge Her methods. Swipe right. Match. Message. Whatsapp. Our text conversations flowed, and when Zoe sent a voice note, I told her her voice would make for a great ringtone, so she sent another of her singing the message acappella style. Her voice gave me goosebumps. It was cute, soothing and full of character, so I phoned her. Remembering the future, somebody asked, "How did you know she was the one?" I replied, "It was the frequency of her voice." Likened to a person tuning an analogue radio in search of their favourite station, Zoe's voice was like searching the airwaves and stumbling upon a "radio station" that played all my favourite music – 528 Hz on my FM dial. We spoke most days and it turns out she also attended Sacred Heart College, an eight-year age gap explaining why we didn't meet until now. A few weeks passed before we met in person. She was intriguing and I was enchanted by her intoxicating personality and beautiful soul. The only cause for concern, the different way we expressed our relationship with God. She was Christian and I was Spiritual. Religious indifference threatened any further romance, but we somehow always found a way back to each other, resolving that it could work. On previous experiences when disclosing religious beliefs, any potential romance came to an abrupt end, leaving me feeling like I had leprosy or was a devil worshipper. We spent more time together and I soon forgot about the pain that had been the source of my suffering for the past four years. Zoe was a healer, heaven sent, a gift from my grandmother who had died in June that year, noting that I met Chloe the same year my grandfather had died. My guardian angels were looking after me, but not without their wicked humour as per the similarities in their names, Zoe and Chloe.

Our last surviving grandparent had been sick for some time. More than the usual old age ailments, she had been depressed since my grandfather's passing. I stopped over to visit and see how she was doing after a morning of hustle. She was in bed and in pain. Sitting by her side, we chatted at length in what was our final conversation. I asked her what she thought about as she lay bedridden all day. "I think about your grandfather, all the wonderful memories he gave me and when he is coming to fetch me." She teared up and spoke about the pain she was in. Even taking her medication was painful, as the bitterness of the capsules burnt her tongue and throat. I tried to distract her with humour, telling her about my new relationship and all its perils. She laughed through the pain. "Whatever happened to that missy from America?" she enquired. More laughter ensued. We chatted for a couple hours, and before leaving I held her hand and told her it's ok to let go, and that there was nothing to fear about death if it meant an end to her suffering. She was taken to hospital the next day and died two days later. After seven years of waiting, she was finally reunited with my grandfather.

Despite the loss of my grandmother, everything was falling into place. Business ventures were progressing, and romantic love seemed possible and felt real. MyDigiVault's achievement in the Innotribe challenge had me speaking to senior executives at a major bank, while Privest Bank was already funding my education initiative. Microsoft BizSpark also invested a significant amount of money to build a prototype for MyDigiVault.

Zoe joked that she was feeling 'broodish'. It was a seed planted in my head, and I watered it every day. She also shared her stance in practicing abstinence. The concept of a 'reborn virgin' baffled me, but after testing her resolve I grew to appreciate her point of view. I had objectified women for the longest time and treated sex as a conquest. And while I had experienced intimacy, my spiritual journey and connection with Zoe had taken intimacy to another level. I had grown to an awareness that women are a portal between the spiritual and physical realm, the only force on earth powerful enough to navigate unborn spirits onto this planet. This realisation made me want to wait until marriage. We were in sync, even noting 'relative age effect' as a consideration for wanting to have a baby in January. "2017?" I proposed. She agreed, before the sobering reality hit: we had to conceive in April 2016, less than six months away. But it didn't faze us. We flirted with having an intimate wedding in March, an idea that stressed my brother's fiancée. Jon and Megan planned to marry in September, so we'd be stealing their thunder. The differing religious beliefs that appeared to be a deal breaker took a backseat as we got to know each other. Feelings escalated on my side and

I faced a choice to resist or surrender. I chose the latter. Mistake? Was it too fast too soon? Perhaps, but I promised God I'd pitch up and be fully present. Zoe was studying part time to get her degree and was a keen traveller with trips to Mozambique and a Contiki European tour planned. I wondered if she noticed me falling in love with her the more time we spent together. Opportunity presented itself and we shared a bed, fighting all temptation to abstain from premarital sex. She was worth the wait. In bed, she tucked her feet between my legs, sending a tingling sensation through my body. I had never felt energy like this before, plus I had all my clothes on! We spoke into the early hours, I shared my dreams and struggles with her, and she in turn shared hers, expressing aspirations of leaving corporate to pursue her own business interests. Perhaps we were a powerful husband-and-wife duo in the making…

But as the year drew to a close, things fell apart. It was just like the Principle of Polarity which described the movement towards opposites as one of a pendulum. What goes up, must come down. I met with Privest Bank for a project update. They were pleased with increased user engagement, but voiced concern as to how I had handled the VAT dispute. While they said no more funds, they later changed their minds. I was so embroiled in the feud with our reward's supplier, I ignored the fact that funds had become available. For months the reward's supplier had been on my back about settling the account, even requesting an acknowledgement of debt (which I later discovered would give them the legal edge) and a payment plan, asking for R50. I replied to their CEO, a techie by background with no people skills, "If I had R50, I'd put petrol in my car and visit a school". It became toxic, email trails back and forth culminated in a showdown after I poked holes in their business. "I will no longer be using your services, please shut down the reward's platform and adjust the invoice accordingly." Shots fired! It made perfect sense, noting that only R3,000 of R50,000 had been redeemed at that stage. The incentive part of programme was a failure, teachers were not claiming their rewards, so the remaining budget could be used to settle the account. Blindsided by my anger, I failed to realise the consequences of my actions and the negative impact to the project's beneficiaries – the teachers. The seriousness of my mistake became apparent only in the review. While we settled the account and completed the 12-month proof-of-concept, I had to wait until February to learn whether Privest Bank wanted to continue funding the project.

On the MyDigiVault front, the prototype was complete after eight weeks of development which equated to more than 30,000 lines of code. Taking delivery exposed a disappointing reality that my expectations and the platform weren't aligned. Confirmation of this misalignment evident when the bank I had been engaging concluded that they wanted to buy licenses, but only when the platform was in a more workable state.

I grew anxious; Zoe and I had been making all these plans to settle down. How was I to provide for her and raise a family with the risks I took and my financial demise? The stance by Privest Bank to wait meant the funding requested was no longer forthcoming. I tossed and turned in bed as before, waking up to cold sweats, the stress and anxiety putting strain on my body and emotional wellbeing. Eczema ravaged my arms and chest. I joked and said I was either developing ulcers or cancer as I experienced pain in my torso area, only made worse by severe constipation. My only relief and joy – Zoe. Just sitting on the couch chatting to her replenished my energy levels and give me hope that everything was going to be ok. A sense of comfort that even prompted an old habit, playing with her ears. And after meeting her family at a braai, I told her I loved her.

December arrived and Megan was turning 30 years old, opting to celebrate it in Durban, throwing an all-white boat party. I was out of cash, but Jon offered to sponsor my travel costs, his generosity most welcomed as Zoe was in Durban for the December holidays. It was a magical three fun-filled days, a much-needed distraction as I waited to learn my fate. We spent a couple nights sleeping on a couch as all the rooms in the penthouse were taken by friends who had paid for accommodation. Zoe didn't seem bothered, but deep down it hurt that I wasn't able to afford getting us a room. Entrepreneurship is anything but glamorous. People will celebrate your success one day and not appreciate the 10 years of struggle, sacrifice, blood, sweat and tears behind the illusion of overnight success. I wrestled with my thoughts, but despair turned to peace as her feet brushed up against my legs as we drifted off to sleep. And before returning to Johannesburg, Zoe told me she loved me.

My heart was smiling again.

CHAPTER 11

SHE GAVE ME A WATCH, WHEN ALL I WANTED WAS SOME OF HER TIME

Chapter 11
SHE GAVE ME A WATCH, WHEN ALL I WANTED WAS SOME OF HER TIME

"I love you" and the thought of raising a family with Zoe fuelled my determination to succeed. I started the year working from an office after years of working from home, joining the software development company I had commissioned to build zibuza.net 2.0.

Zoe had some American Pie moments herself as I teased her about having facial hair, which wasn't even there. Before meeting for lunch, she visited the salon to wax, and in haste they removed the wax, pulling the skin off her upper lip. I needed to be careful what I joked about, but thought the gesture to look her best was adorable. Zoe grew on me; there was an inquisitive nature about her, an openness and willingness to grow which was appealing. I observed her joyous mood in the mornings, whistling and singing while she brushed her teeth, did her hair and put makeup on. She joked about the rings under her eyes being the reason she always wore makeup, but it didn't bother me, she was beautiful regardless. I saw her insecurities, her flaws and faults, the pain she was hiding and the emotional baggage she was carrying. She was enough; I loved her - warts and all. Perhaps most disturbing was an argument we had where Zoe expressed her unease at me playing with her ears, especially in public. How a gesture of affection became the source of tension and accusations of smothering baffled me, so I probed for a logical explanation. The lingering ghosts of apartheid that taught us to hate ourselves explained it best. As kids, hair probably mattered more than skin colour. For boys, we would just keep our hair short. For girls, it was a case of blow drying and painfully brushing 'unmanageable' hair, ironing, hair relaxing and in more recent times, GHDs, Brazilian hair straightening treatments and human hair weaves – the most sought-after include Brazilian, Peruvian, Indian, Malaysian and Eurasian hair. Zoe's unease at me playing with her ears was down to her fear that her weave would be dislodged in the

Chapter 11: She gave me a Watch, when all I Wanted was some of her Time

process. How sad is it though, that by global standards where oppressive practices have been abolished, that our definition of beauty is still measured by European standards, whereby a profit is derived? I was left speechless by her answer before jokingly replying that I would only play with her ears in private.

There was a noticeable shift in my approach to relationships from 'get to know somebody and see if it works before deciding' to 'decide, get to know somebody and make it work'. Although I must confess, there was now doubt as to Zoe being the right person to start a family with – would she pass the same insecurities on to our kids as the ones she had about her hair?

Zoe met more of my family at one of the many birthday get-togethers, her infectious personality and polite manners noted by my aunts as they concluded – yes, this one's a keeper. My family can be quite intimidating, mostly intentionally, but even on the occasions when they were on their best behaviour – as was the case with my mother when she called Zoe "Chloe". It was after lunch and all the ladies were gathered in the kitchen doing the dishes and preparing dessert. I'm not sure what the conversation was about, but the incident occurred just as I was entering the kitchen – awkward silence filled the room and I turned and walked out immediately, my mother consoling Zoe with a hug and apology!

The day ended on a high however, with Zoe surprising me with a Christmas gift – a watch. While grateful, I shared the Christmas tale of how our watches were stolen as kids, and how an uncle gave us watches in recent years, only to find they were stolen property. He was a panel beater and, upon discovering the watches in a client's car, kept them and then distributed them as Christmas gifts. His strong religious beliefs were not lost on me as I remembered the conflict within me that grew as a child as I witnessed the hypocrisy of God's most loyal and obedient followers. It even prompted me to state that Christianity was born out of Neanderthal ways.

I was out of line and disrespectful. If our relationship stood any chance, let alone raise children together, I needed to change my views towards organised religion, and even considered going to church with Zoe in addition to the time and effort I was already investing in my spiritual growth. Maybe this watch would be my lucky charm. Zoe had plans with her girlfriends on Friday night so we agreed to meet on Saturday. I went to gym Saturday morning followed by lunch with Danny and Blessed, gym buddies for over 7 years. I drove all the way to Rivonia, 30km away twice a week just to train with them. Our friendship, like countless others a sign of how far we have come as a country. Danny is a stockbroker in his 50s, white. Blessed is an IT Consultant in his 30s and from Zimbabwe, black. We are indeed a rainbow nation or, like Danny explains it – my eyes are blue, yours are brown, we both use them to see – at which point I have to remind him that my eyes are in fact hazel. At lunch, I shared news about the love I had found and the plans we had made. They thought I was crazy, which didn't come as a surprise; most things about my way of life disturbed them. "You should get a private investigator and find out more about her," they chirped out of concern. I found it insulting and felt the energy shift from positive to negative. Why were they trying to ruin the happiness that had eluded me for all these years? The food had yet to arrive at our table when Zoe sent a message, "Hey babe, I only got home at 5 am, can we please take a rain check?" You can always rely on banter from the boys. Danny was on que to remark, "I've got the number of a good P.I." I felt disappointed after looking forward to seeing her and then remembered Zoe mention that our relationship came with such ease, and that she was waiting for our first fight. I thought it an opportune moment to scratch this item off her list, so I replied, "I worked Friday night to free up time to spend with you". And when she apologised, I followed up, "How would you feel if I was the one out until 5 am and cancelled on you", to which she replied, "I'd be furious!" and apologised again. Just to make sure the 'fight' was serious enough, I ignored her and only after a few days did I change my Whatsapp profile to a picture of us from our time in Durban to signal that all was forgiven – welcome to the modern age of dating. Zoe said she missed me. Great, everything was going according to plan.

We met early that evening at a coffee shop in Rosebank. I had the most terrible day and was frustrated at the slow progress of our new zibuza. net platform and the pending Privest Bank decision. As I made my way to the coffee shop, I had to remind myself not to be miserable, but failed to hide my frustration, exposing her to my impossible argumentative self, challenging everything she said. Without warning, she broke up with me,

Chapter 11: She gave me a Watch, when all I Wanted was some of her Time

then explained she thought she was ready for a relationship but wasn't and still wanted her freedom. She didn't want the responsibility of being in a relationship or being accountable to anybody where she'd have to explain herself. I tried to downplay our fight from the weekend, but it didn't seem to matter; her mind had been made. The final blow: she said the difference in our beliefs was still a deal breaker. My body language showed defeat as she held back the tears, clenching her jaw. The watch that was my lucky charm now choked my wrist. We lingered for a few moments of awkward silence before I dragged myself off the couch to leave. We made our way to the parking lot and hugged before going our separate ways. What the freaking hell just happened? I removed the watch from my wrist and sat in the car for what seemed like hours.

The breakup sparked a flood of memories from the pain of losing Chloe. There were unresolved issues I had been avoiding. I wanted to apologise for my reckless actions, but couldn't; it wouldn't have been sincere. Like a shameful secret that perpetuates lie after lie, it left me burdened with guilt. Even though I had deleted all our photos off Facebook, I still kept copies on a hard drive, along with a sex tape we had made. Long-distance relationships call for some creativity when you're apart for long periods at a time. I didn't even realize the seriousness of what I had held onto until hearing about 'revenge porn' in the news where bitter exes upload explicit material to humiliate and intimidate their former lovers. I could never resort to that level of evil, but somehow couldn't delete it. Perhaps I'd watch it again on my deathbed, I reasoned. Perhaps it was the reason holding me back...? Sense prevailed, so I deleted the sex tape. A huge relief as the burden was lifted. I sent Chloe an apology via email, acknowledging my reckless behaviour and faults, asking for nothing back as a gesture of sincerity. She responded a few hours later calling me an inhumane evil woman abuser psychopath, wishing all the ills of the world on me, including that I be alone for an eternity. She was right; as much as I was capable of doing good in this world, I was also capable of evil and destruction.

Divine dichotomy, a painful fact to acknowledge as I owned up to the challenge of choosing to do good every day, taking responsibility and being fully accountable for my actions.

Default protocol for breakups is a total disconnection from the aggressor, but I stayed in touch with Zoe, even agreeing to a friendship. We still spent time together, still showed the same affection towards each other, and on my birthday I teased her saying that if this is what friendship entails, then I was all for it. It was the last time I'd ever see her. In the weeks that followed I asked her to be my valentine, but she was away on a cruise in Mozambique, sending me a Whatsapp message, "Happy Valentine's Day". How boring I thought, and replied later that night, "I pray to God about you, Happy Valentine's Day". No reply. A few weeks passed and when we chatted I asked her what she thought of my message. She felt I was just saying so to convince her to get back together. I was angry; the gesture was sincere. I had been on a soul-searching mission and prayed, asking God for patience, understanding and strength when it came to her. I tried and tried again to make plans with Zoe, only for them never to materialise, even offering to help review her study notes and quiz her as she prepped for exams. Tension mounted as I felt her slipping away, pointing out that we went from a relationship with intentions to get married, to a friendship, to acquaintances, a pattern that was leading to nothingness. Zoe apologised, saying the last thing she wanted was to make an enemy of me. It was the furthest thing from my mind. I just wanted some of her time.

I would dream of her. Finding myself on a bed, surrounded by familiar people. I was arguing with a stranger, a woman. And in the heat of the argument, I noticed the woman was Zoe. She reached out to calm me, drew me closer and put her arm around me to lay in a loving embrace. Peace and bliss replaced anger.

After three months of waiting, Privest Bank reached a conclusion: they no longer wanted to support or fund zibuza.net. Their reason: broken trust. As a final gesture, they offered to fund a transition period, paying for 12-months' licensing to give me time to find another funder. I had already started development on version 2.0 of the platform and wasn't prepared to work another 12 months with the reward's supplier. Coincidently, the amounts for a 12-months' license and building the new platform were the same, so I secured quotes from the current suppliers and planned to use the money to pay the new developers. With no trust, Privest Bank said they wanted to pay the money directly to the suppliers. It was only at this point that I disclosed news of using the money to fund the new platform. The head of their CSI called, "Malcolm, what is wrong with you?" I echoed his sentiment.

He then withdrew their offer to transition and left me with parting words of advice, "You work six steps ahead of us and don't take us along with you, and that will cost you dearly in any future engagement". The cost of my mistake was R2,5 million. Lesson learnt.

With no money left, my only saving grace was the sales commission from the stationery manufacturer. It bought me another six months to dream.

Chloe's words of inhumane evil woman abuser psychopath were still lingering in my thoughts, so I resolved not to subject Zoe to the same fate, sending her a parting message of well wishes and safe travels as she embarked on her European adventure. No reply.

A week later, notifications from my Instagram account showed that Zoe had followed me and liked several of my pictures. Strange; make nothing of it. The next day, a friend request on Facebook. Maybe she was trying to send me a message after finding herself in Europe? I accepted and followed back. She posted daily of her adventure, tourist attractions and group pics with other girls. But as the days went by, tagged pictures suggested signs of a romance. Was I seeing things? I had been on a Contiki Greek Island tour some 10 years prior and knew all about the hook up shenanigans that the Contiki experience offered. Day after day Facebook taunted me with more pictures. The final straw, a picture of her in a romantic pose on a gondola in Venice, sitting positioned between his legs as he held her, their smiles a dagger to my heart. My emotions raged. I didn't know whether to cry, punch a hole through the wall or be happy for her. I couldn't sleep, my brain sore from trying to process the infinite data streams of potential future realities. Would she go there, would he come here, do I share the pitfalls of long-distance relationships with her? This is the gift and curse nature of the way my brain processed information and emotions. Great for business, painful for romance. I'm a seasoned business executive come awkward teenager. My only relief and logical reaction, unfriending her on Facebook and unfollowing her on

Instagram at 2:45 am. In this moment of strife, the source of my lingering pain was revealed. Emotional attachment.

Nothing humbles a person more than the revelations that surface from the subconscious mind. It's an awareness that is painful yet liberating. I discovered the difference between love and emotional attachment. Love is a positive feeling 'towards' somebody, whereas attachment is an 'emotional need' for somebody; it was self-centred and only considered my needs. It was a case of needs versus neediness – what a contrast to expose the torture I had subjected myself and others to over the years. An online blog explained it:

"Needs are normal, valid, important; present in everyone, including healthy, successful people; necessary to survive and thrive; best met by taking responsibility, initiative; unmet needs stimulate action; most effectively met by being assertive; met needs results in contentment and one's ability to get needs met attracts others.

Neediness comes from desperation, helplessness; driven by emotional deficits; externalised problem and solution; results in helpless/victim position; is insatiable, always needing more and results in repelling others."

Knowing this has made all the difference. While I loved Winnie, Chloe and Zoe, there was also an unhealthy emotional attachment. I was making them responsible for fulfilling my emotional needs instead of owning that responsibility. I was relinquishing my creative power and resourcefulness which made it seem all the more difficult to let go. On some level, I was looking to them to make me whole. My desire to hold on to the relationships was less about love and more about my own fears, loneliness, and desperation to have my emotional needs met.

Is it still love if the person you choose doesn't choose you?
And would you still stick around and just be friends?

The heartbreak, inspiration for a poem she would never get to hear.

Chapter 11: She gave me a Watch, when all I Wanted was some of her Time

Would you believe me if I told you that I loved you before I met you?
Don't focus on what it means to be loved by me,
your walls of protection to keep you safe are impenetrable.
Instead, think about how you perceive and feel time.
A construct that keeps you sane but doesn't serve you.
Linear, logical, sequential — cause and effect.
Now, imagine that time didn't exist and everything that ever was and ever will be is happening all at once. Feel every emotion in a spectrum of feelings happening all at once, the highest high and lowest low.
Conscious Energy, raw and endless.
What if time and polarity existed just so we could find meaning in life's experiences?
For our souls to appreciate God's creation.
If this was true, then our souls have been dancing together throughout the ages,
Unconditionally loving each other at a spiritual level.
A bond so strong and trusting,
we would cause each other heartbreak through the millennia,
just so we can know and appreciate love again.
We would separate just to experience yearning, all to know and appreciate love again. We would find other lovers again and again through human experience,
just to know and appreciate the love we share for each other.
And if all this was true, then perhaps our souls reacquainting in this lifetime is why the connection I feel for you is so strong and stubborn.
My pace too fast? Too much too soon?
It's just me remembering you from past lifetimes. You remind me of so many things my soul has experienced,
people I hold dear and even those I dislike.
Perhaps you not loving me in this lifetime means we can know and appreciate love again in our next lifetime. So, do you believe me when I tell you that I loved you before I even met you?

Indigo Child

For a year that brought with it so much promise, I had lost everything.

CHAPTER 12
I'LL BE HAPPY WHEN...

Chapter 12
I'LL BE HAPPY WHEN...

I'll be happy when... is a game I love to play. I'll be happy when I'm successful with a massive bank balance. I'll be happy when I find a soulmate for love and companionship to start a family. I'll be happy when I have all the answers to all the questions to make the world a better place for all.

Like all stories there is a structure, an introduction, the main body and an ending. In my case, there is no ending, perhaps true to my rebellious nature to bend the rules, but more so in that my journey is still unfolding. Having lost everything, I have a story to tell. Writing a book forms part of a bucket list of things to do and places to see in this lifetime. But like so many other aspirations in life, I am guilty of linking it to some future event or achievement that may or may not happen. My trigger for writing a book was first building successful businesses to have the credibility and authority that comes along with it to justify sharing my story. This is the nature of our lives and storytelling: we only tell stories after the fact, then hero worship at the achievements of others while ignoring our own call to adventure, never realising the greatness within us, no matter how big or small, no matter the outcome. I am inspired by those around me and the events that have shaped and influenced my life to share my story now as it is still unfolding, risking the potential for ridicule, judgement and persecution, while also aware of the opportunity to inspire, entertain and share knowledge of the lessons learnt.

Do you love me? I am deeply flawed and a disaster in the making. Do you hate me? I am capable of good and greatness that is powerful beyond measure. Of all the complexities and mysteries in life, I've learnt that choosing and taking action is based on only two factors: fear or love.

I choose love.

PART 2

INTO THE DEPTHS OF DARKNESS

CHAPTER 13

THE COLOURED DELUSION

Chapter 13
THE COLOURED DELUSION

*The world as WE have created it is a process of OUR thinking.
It cannot be changed without changing our thinking"
~Albert Einstein*

"Pseudoscience describes any belief system or methodology which tries to gain legitimacy by wearing the trappings of science, but fails to abide by the rigorous methodology and standards of evidence that are the marks of true science."

"Scientific racism is the use of ostensibly scientific or pseudo-scientific techniques and hypotheses to support or justify the belief in racism, racial inferiority, racialism, racial superiority, or alternatively the practice of classifying individuals of different phenotypes into discrete races."

"Apartheid: an Afrikaans word meaning 'separateness', or 'the state of being apart', was a system of racial segregation in South Africa enforced through legislation by the National Party (NP), the governing party from 1948 to 1994."

If you want to understand my anger, pain, defiance and anti-establishment attitude, you need to understand the world I was born into – an apartheid state. Below are some of the acts taken from the Nelson Mandela Centre of Memory that were compiled and authored by Padraig O' Malley. A more extensive list can be found on their website.

But first, thoughts are real forces and words have real power:

Morality: *principles concerning the distinction between right and wrong or good and bad behaviour.*

Immorality: *not conforming to accepted standards of morality.*

Chapter 13: The Coloured Delusion

Prohibition: *the action of forbidding something, especially by law.*

Forbid: *refuse to allow (something).*

Physical appearance: *defining traits or features about your body.*

Social acceptability: *the ability to accept or to tolerate differences and diversity in other people or groups of people.*

Aspire: *direct one's hopes or ambitions towards achieving something.*

Invalid: *a person made weak or disabled by illness or injury.*

1949. Prohibition of Mixed Marriages Act No 55
This act forbade marriages between Whites and non-Whites.

1950. Immorality Amendment Act No 21
This act forbade any sexual relations between Whites and non-Whites.

1950. Population Registration Act No 30
The South African population now became divided into three racial groups: 'White', 'Black' ('African', 'Native' and/or 'Bantu') and 'Coloured'; the last of which was further subcategorised into 'Cape Malay', 'Griqua', 'Indian', 'Chinese' and 'Cape Coloured'. Classification was determined according to physical appearance and social acceptability.

1950. Group Areas Act No 41
Urban areas were to be divided into racially segregated zones "where members of one specific race alone could live and work". Group areas were created "for the exclusive ownership and occupation of a designated group". It further became "a criminal offence for a member of one racial group to reside on or own land in an area set aside by proclamation for another race".

1953. Reservation of Separate Amenities Act No 49
This act "sought to create separate social environments for the White and other population groups".

1953. Bantu Education Act
This act further segregated the already segregated educational system of South Africa. "Blacks were not to aspire to certain positions in society and so education for such positions was not deemed necessary".

1968. Prohibition of Mixed Marriages Amendment Act No 21. This act "declared that the marriage of a male South African citizen and a woman of a different race which had been contracted abroad was invalid in South Africa".

In Sunday school, we were taught that we are all created as equals in the image of God. I think about all the negative words used in these acts and the lingering impact it has had on our society. If the Bible is the final authority on all religious matters, how is it so ambiguous that theologians could justify that it was God's will to separate the races and forbid them to mix? Beyond segregation, how did lawmakers justify black people being stripped of their citizenship to receive inferior education and medical care services, and severely limit our participation in the economy? From a quantum physics perspective, if our neural pathways of habitual thought form our beliefs, and our beliefs set our expectations, and our expectations manifest our reality in a physical realm of infinite possibilities, then those who control our thoughts, control our realities.

Our country's history is a peculiar one in that it is the only country in the world, under apartheid, where an oppressive government managed to create an artificial race and culture.

The sad reality is that while we are 22 years into a democratic society, the legacy of apartheid is still alive and well. Despite the Truth & Reconciliation process as well as other interventions like Affirmative Action, Black Economic Empowerment and Broad-Based Black Economic Empowerment, there is still huge economic disparity and no intervention to FIX THE PSYCHE of those of us subjected to many decades of pseudo-scientific brainwashing.

I am extremely proud of my heritage, but I despise being referred to as a coloured. Not so much as a people, but more in the way that 'we' were defined under the apartheid acts and how it continues to define and limit 'us'.

Chapter 13: The Coloured Delusion

*"Emancipate yourselves from mental slavery.
None but ourselves can free our minds."
~ Bob Marley*

CHAPTER 14
THE STORY BEHIND THE STORY

Chapter 14
THE STORY BEHIND THE STORY

My known mixed heritage dates as far back as the 1800s, so diverse and rich it is sad to think that much of it remains a mystery that is lost to time.

From my father's side, it starts with the union of my great-grandparents Leung Lok Wangon and Francis Milton. Wangon hailed from Canton in China, leaving home at 16 years of age on a boat to arrive after two years at sea on the shores of South Africa. The story is unclear as to why he left home – it was either in search of gold or to escape the turmoil in China. Francis hailed from Colesburg in the Karoo, her parents a Scotsman and a Hottentot. They would birth six children, one of them being John William Mooi aka Oupa Johnny. The other notable facts: our surname and the pencil test. There are several versions as to why Wangon would change our surname to Mooi. One speaks about the need to protect his family as the Chinese were the smallest minority group at the time and faced severe discrimination. The other, Francis was not happy with a Chinese surname and wanted a good Catholic surname.

A family stamp, an heirloom consisting of three chops containing Chinese characters translates into "Leung Lok Mei Sui Gin".

Leung = Clan of Leung; Lok = 6; Mei = Rose; Sui = Book and Gin = Most learned, most respected. I suspect that the Afrikaner at Home Affairs could not understand Wangon's broken English accent and interpreted Mei for Mooi.

The pencil test was used to determine racial identity with the aim of splitting existing communities and families along perceived racial lines. This is the invisible power of pseudo-science. At such a young and impressionable age before even interacting with other racial groups,

Chapter 14: The Story behind the Story

I was concerned as to the curly "kroes" nature of my hair, asking my older cousins when I would grow my straighter Chinese hair. Mary Leah Basing aka Grandma ran away from home in Beira, Mozambique at the tender age of 10 to eventually attend a Catholic Convent School in Potchefstroom. Her father was a white Portuguese sugar cane farmer, her mother a black Mozambican. She would claim she ran away from home because her father murdered her mother, but it was more likely that after her mother passed away for reasons unknown, her father would marry a white woman with whom she didn't get along.

From my mother's side, the lineage traces back to Holland, Indonesia and Sweden. Manun and Ganun Jakoet were brothers who arrived in South Africa in the early 1870s from Surabaya in Indonesia. They settled in Kimberley in the Northern Cape where they worked in the diamond mines. As far as surnames go, they would also anglicise their surname to Jacobs to be more socially acceptable as well as take advantage of the associated opportunities that came with an English surname. The brothers would go on to father up to 16 children. Manun and his wife Rakeeba would have nine children, Gesant Jacobs the most notable as he would father Clifford Leon Smith with Maggie Du Preez (née Smith). Maggie's grandfather hailed from the Netherlands and his wife from Saint Helena, a volcanic tropical island in the South Atlantic Ocean, 4,000 kilometres east of Rio de Janeiro and 1,950 kilometres west of the Cunene River. Maggie's mother Dina was mixed with Hottentot and Swedish. She grew up in Paarl in the Western Cape before moving up to Johannesburg. As my auntie Edna (Oupa Cliffie's sister) explains it, this Swedish connection is where some of our family members get their blonde hair and blue eyes from. Maggie aka Ouma Lena passed away five months after I was born in June of 1979. While I do not remember anything about her, she did give me my second name Roger, after Roger Moore – she was a big fan of the James Bond movies. While both my parents are fair skinned, Ouma Lena was 'pleased' that I was born with brown skin and dark hair. Her counterpart, Ouma Bella held the opposite sentiment. Christabelle van der Hoeven, aka Ouma Bella, was the daughter of Arend van der Hoeven and Sarah Job. Sarah was a Hottentot from the Northern Cape and Arend was a baker from the Netherlands who made his way to South Africa in the 1800s in search of riches in the diamond mines of the Northern Cape. While Ouma

Bella never married, she would give birth to three daughters – my grandmother Yvonne, Eunice and Esmé. Esmé would later change her name to Hadia when getting married and converting from Christianity to Islam. My bloodline spans Chinese, Portuguese, Scottish, Hottentot, Black, Dutch, Swedish and Indonesian descent. Their arrival in South Africa perhaps in search of riches in the form of gold, diamonds and new opportunities or perhaps to escape the turmoil in their homelands. Like the ships that took enslaved Africans across the Atlantic to the Americas with iron collars around their necks, their hands in chains and their feet in shackles, my ancestors would arrive back in Africa to also be subjected to slavery – mental slavery. In just one generation, we would lose our mixed heritage identities, connections and culture to be classified and take on the assumed identity of a coloured.

CHAPTER 15

INTELLECTUAL EN-SLAVE-MENT

Chapter 15
INTELLECTUAL EN-SLAVE-MENT

"There is no place for [the Bantu] in the European community above the level of certain forms of labour. What is the use of teaching the Bantu child mathematics when it cannot use it in practice?"
– Hendrik Verwoerd

"Leaders of white public opinion, take every opportunity to present us in the world as sub-human beings incapable of assimilating civilisation. This matter of dwarfing our personality and trying to make us believe that we are nobodies is the worst sin the white man has committed against Africans."
– Chief Luthuli

Bantu Education was potentially the most disabling of all the acts introduced under the apartheid regime. Intentionally structured to produce a low-paid, labour-intensive workforce to promote a social order that would keep people of colour at the lower echelons of the labour market, as well as perpetuate the essential idea that future generations understand that they are unequal, inferior and different.

The act was repealed in the year I was born by the Education and Training Act of 1979, but the system of racially segregated education continued until 1994 when segregation became unconstitutional under the Interim Constitution, with most sections of the Education and Training Act only repealed by the South African Schools Act of 1996.

It saddens me deeply to think about all the lost potential, lost dreams and aspirations of so many people.

Chapter 15: Intellectual En-Slave-ment

The child in me thinks back to Sunday school and wonders if these are the sins that Jesus Christ had come to die for. And like Jesus who expressed His feelings of abandonment to God during His crucifixion, that same child would go on to leave the church and become an atheist for two decades, wondering why God would forsake us and allow such atrocities to ever happen.

Memories take me back to London: *"18 June 2000, Sunday. Went to a BBQ at Debbie's... interesting afternoon, very interesting!!!"* An intense debate questioned the very nature of organised religion. It was the first time I had heard the argument that religion was nothing but a tool to control and pacify the masses to prevent chaos and preserve the interests of the elite and upper echelons of society, a system built on white male supremacy.

"Slaves, obey your earthly masters in everything; and do it, not only when their eye is on you and to win their favour, but with sincerity of heart and reverence for the Lord." (Colossians 3:22)

Surely the oppressor and the oppressed cannot pray to the same 'Saviour'?

Previously blasphemous and off-limits questions flooded my mind and were up for discussion. In our Anglican church, Jesus is bronzed, nailed to a cross. At the Chapel in Sacred Heart College, wall murals of Jesus' life depict him as white. Is my saviour white? Jesus' twelve disciples were Peter, James, John, Andrew, Philip, Bartholomew, Thomas, Matthew, James, Thaddaeus, Simon and Judas. Was it just the time and location Jesus found Himself in to choose Caucasian males or is this just down to the translation to English? Would 'Thabo' or 'Jabu' be worthy of His company? And if Jesus had black disciples, would people still listen to Him? Why weren't there any female disciples? Did His journey represent what was happening in Africa, Asia and South America at the time? And what of 'coloured' people; did we even exist 2,000 years ago?

Did Stockholm syndrome nullify our anger and inevitable retaliation brought on by the crusades and colonialism, leading us to develop sypathetic sentiments towards our oppressors to embrace their way of life, their God, to embrace their opinions of us and our place in society? It was an afternoon of intellectually engaging conversations, Henessy, flirtation and conspiracy theories that also touched on the industries driving the global economies. Take pharmaceuticals as an example, with annual revenues reaching nearly one trillion U.S. dollars: would it be in the best interests of pharmaceutical companies to explore unlocking the body's native repair and regenerative systems for natural healing at the risk of forgoing these annual revenues? There is certainly a pattern of sorts when delving further into these trillion-dollar industries, especially their power and influence over governments in setting laws and regulations.

For me, the one that stood out was the alcohol industry. It peaked my curiosity as a child observing my father and uncles. It wasn't just our family, alcohol seemed to be the general focus point for all social interactions in our community. Once we came of age, it become a part of our lifestyle too. How did this unhealthy relationship with alcohol become so ingrained in our lives? Is there a connection between our country's past and its affinity to alcohol? Going through some online archives in recent times, my suspicions are confirmed. Historian, Noor Nieftagodien says that the culture of drinking in black and coloured communities is a result of the way people's lives were controlled – how they were defined, where they could go and what jobs they could have – it was controlled in a way which almost bizarrely supported inebriation. He goes on to refer to the dop (tot) system that thrived on farms where farmers would pay their workers in the form of wine, giving rise to endemic alcoholism, a system and culture of inebriation that keeps reproducing itself. Then there were isidakwa (drunkards). Mines used drink as a form of reward.

Liquor made migrant workers more prepared to accept their miserable lives which centred around work, sleep and leisure (drink).

More than intellectual enslavement, it's profitability over our humanity.

CHAPTER 16
FAILURE TO LAUNCH

Chapter 16
FAILURE TO LAUNCH

I've lived in Riverlea my entire life, a coloured township located in the southwest of Johannesburg. Surrounded by three abandoned mine dumps, our community is the legacy of colonial mining and apartheid settlement patterns intentionally designed to alienate and segregate communities. With only two entry/exit points to limit our mobility in the event of an uprising, Riverlea was built by a malicious apartheid government that dumped people where no one else wanted to live under the 1950 Group Areas Act No 41.

Johannesburg mine dumps are man-made dumps that resemble huge molehill shapes which provide a distinctively beautiful skyline that glows a golden yellow colour in the sun and a blazing red colour at dusk.

George Harrison Park, the site of the discovery of the largest gold field on earth is less than two kilometres from my home. In August and September, winds spray 'gold' dust into the air to symbolise the birth of Johannesburg, the City of Gold. Sadly, it is not gold dust but rather the residue of decades of mining, containing traces of everything from copper and lead to radioactive cyanide and uranium. Our sub-human status meant we were not afforded an environmental impact assessment which would expose the health hazards and associated diseases like chronic nasal allergies, allergic rhinitis and sinuses, asthma, bronchitis, eczema, head sores, rashes and skin diseases that have plagued our community and are ubiquitous across all age groups. As a child, I can remember white blemishes that appeared on our skin and we had no escape from the seasonal chest and nasal infections. Riverlea, it's a complex love affair. Despite my indifference and disconnection from the community that raised and shaped me, at 37 years of age I am still living with my parents in the house I grew up in. Most would attribute this oddity as my failure to launch, confirmation of my susceptibility to emotional attachment and reluctance to leave my 'mother's womb'. Few would understand the reasons why...

CHAPTER 17
THE ENABLERS

Chapter 17
THE ENABLERS

In Malcolm Gladwell's book Outliers, he tells the story of Italian immigrants from Roseto Valfortore who settled in a small town in Pennsylvania, which they named Roseto. What was interesting about their community is that hardly any of the men suffered from heart disease compared to other communities. Extensive studies were done to understand why the community from Roseto was not prone to heart disease, including their physical makeup, culture, lifestyle, among all other possible factors. It was eventually concluded that Roseto, an outlier for being different from the norm when it came to heart disease, was healthy not because of individual efforts to stay healthy, but because the people lived in a supportive environment surrounded by their close friends and family members, often multiple generations under one roof.

Being an entrepreneur is like jumping off a cliff, assembling a plane and learning to fly before hitting the ground. Living at home my whole life has certainly made all the difference in allowing me to live my dream and jump off that cliff many times over. My parents' unconditional love and unwavering support has given me an infinite supply of belief and the resolve to persist through all the adversity that comes with being an entrepreneur living on the edge of chaos. An entrepreneur's journey is a treacherous one, and the ups and downs of such an undertaking are astounding – loneliness, hope, depression, anger, joy, doubt, excitement, stress, love, confusion, passion, sacrifice, confidence, financial strain, introversion, break-ups, forced extraversion, anxiety, success, failure, more failure, clarity, setbacks – it is a plethora of gut-wrenching feelings and emotions that happen all at once, and with great intensity! It affects every aspect of your being and is potentially the most humbling of forces that will test your resolve and push you out of your comfort zone. It's like eating broken glass and learning to enjoy the taste of your own blood. In the spirit of being open and vulnerable, financially I went from earning amazing sales commissions to going without a salary since

Chapter 17: The Enablers

November 2009 to make it 78 months and counting, with all the money I've made along the way being re-invested back into the business ventures. And it's the small things we take for granted that hurt the most. For instance, worn out underpants and holes in my socks as I watched people 'progress' in life: getting married, buying a house, starting a family, promotions at work, while all I ever seem to experience is failure and lack. "How much more do I have to give of myself?" has been top of my mind for many years now. It feels like showering in doubt and moisturising myself in hopelessness most days. Romantically, it is hard to imagine starting and maintaining a relationship with anybody under these conditions, and when love has blessed me, feelings of inadequacy that I am not relationship material are amplified and only made worse by my passive aggressive anger. While I've mastered the art of a minimalistic lifestyle, I have suffered in a lonely struggle to find connection and companionship. Choices that from the surface level render me a conservative dull guy, drama free and socially inept – all chemistry killers, to a deeper awakening that transcends the material façade of modern relationships where pleasure can be found in just the time spent with somebody, just being fully present or expressing feelings through creativity. I recall the anguish of deciding whether to buy Zoe flowers for her birthday or put petrol in my car to get to meetings. And I couldn't afford roses so in addition to the bouquet of flowers, I made custom birthday vouchers that she could redeem – ranging from a foot massage to writing her a poem, only to be humbled by the realization that my struggle wasn't her struggle. She needed more, and deserved more than I could offer. Will it all be worth it or have I wasted away my 30s? By traditional standards, revenue and traction, it would lean to the latter – 78 (and counting) salary months I can never get back, pensions and investments cashed in, any progress made exposing the dog-eat-dog nature of business making it difficult to trust anyone. Am I being paranoid? Experience would disagree. But do I have a choice? Business is all about relationships and networks – great ideas and extreme efficiency still make me a single point of failure, a liability for investment. Somebody once told me you can measure a person's aptitude for entrepreneurship with one question – what is their threshold for pain, both emotional and physical pain? Emotionally, I have suffered for long periods with depression, often struggling to get myself out of bed. And while it never reached serious thoughts of suicide, I've often questioned my self-worth and whether anybody would miss me if I was dead.

Physically, this has translated into eczema breakouts on my body, prolonged constipation and abdominal pain.

I'm not even ashamed to admit that I've cried several times, albeit in my sleep – if you recall, we don't cry openly in our family.

The unconditional love and unwavering support from my parents is the single biggest factor that has gotten me this far. As my journey unfolds, I get a sense that my parents live vicariously through me, ever-patient supporters rooting for my success. Perhaps an opportunity to experience success in realising dreams that were unavailable to them, like so many others during the height of an apartheid era.

My father shares an early memory of a trip he took with his mom to Fordsburg to visit family. They returned home as usual on a double-decker tram. People of colour were only allowed to sit on the balcony, not inside, which was reserved for whites only. He recalls that on this particular day it had been raining. The conductor approached them and said, "The master can go sit inside". My grandma was very outspoken and replied, "What do you mean the master, he's my son?" They were both eventually allowed to go inside. As far as skin complexion goes, my grandma was dark and my father is fair. This was the logic that the conductor used, based on law, to determine who could sit where on a public mode of transport.

My father had an ear for music and was a talented singer. At 12 years of age, he had formed his first band, called the Blue Jean Boys. Their influences were Elvis Presley among other Blues artists. They would sing on the weekends at local dances during the intervals and he would go on to audition for a spot in a coon carnival band that would tour overseas. He made the cut, only to lose his spot after his voice broke as he entered puberty. He then taught himself to play the guitar – a gift from his father. By the time he reached high school there were quite a few teachers immigrating to other countries, warning them to get out of the country if they ever wanted to advance in life. He finished school in 1962 and spent the December holidays partying up a storm. A family friend approached my grandma and enquired if she knew any fair of complexion persons for a job opening to work at a clothing

Chapter 17: The Enablers

manufacturing factory as a dispatch clerk. Grandma took no nonsense and so on January 2nd 1963, my father still hungover, with his fair skin, got the job. He would work there for the next 47 years before retiring in 2010. The company would change ownership five times and he would be promoted to warehouse manager and key holder during this time. How he could work for one company his whole life is beyond me, as I enquire why and how it came to be that he never pursued his dreams. "There were very limited options and my priority was to take care of my family," he replies. His story is like many others at this time in our country's history; people with potential but very limited opportunities – at 18, he bought himself an electric guitar. It cost R36 and he'd pay R2/week for three months before being able to take it home. His love for music would see him a founding member of the band, the Square Sircles. The band was a hit at local dances and toured parts of the country before securing a gig to be the opening act for the Flames before SA's biggest band went abroad. The highlight of the Square Sircle's history was signing a recording contract with EMI Music where they spent several recording sessions in a studio putting together an album. Sadly, the band broke up after six years together and the album was never released.

My mother's early days seem to have come and gone without much hassle – perhaps a life of fair complexion and privilege afforded to her by her father, a doctor. Her life took on new meaning when she answered her call to adventure and broke away from the traditional path to become one of the founding members of Little People Preschool and Care Centre. A group of four ladies established an early childhood development centre after recognising the need in our community for young children to have a good foundation for future learning before commencing formal education. They started off in a church hall in Coronationville in 1985 offering a half-day service that catered for 40 children between the ages of 3 and 6. Their dream was to build premises that would be more conducive for young people to learn, grow and develop. I had just started 'big school' and did not understand the significance of the work they were doing. Instead, I remember harbouring anger towards my mother as her aspirations and dream came at the expense of us being a single-income household for many years to come. Their dream was eventually realised when acquiring property in Riverlea Ext. 2 after raising funds, obtaining a loan and receiving sponsorship. Construction of the building began in 1990 and they were finally able to move in in 1995. The history of 'Little People' has a rich tapestry, woven by the many adversities they've had to endure over the years. In 1993, the church ceiling collapsed and they had to move to St. Joseph's Home in Sophiatown. St. Joseph's Home assisted with accommodation and transportation as a goodwill gesture for the preschool having sponsored several children from their orphanage. In 1994, they relocated to the Coronationville Recreation Centre, and in September that year the centre was petrol bombed during a community demonstration. Once again they were forced to move, this time to the old Catholic church across the road. Little People celebrated its 31st anniversary in 2016 and provides a full-day service that caters for 110 young children between the ages of 2 and 6, with a staff compliment that has increased from 5 to 16. The preschool, like Pinetree High School (PHS) in Yeoville is an oasis in the desert, another example of what is possible, regardless of the location or financial means. As far as excellence goes, the preschool was acknowledged in 2013 for best practice, adhering to the ethos of the Batho Pele principles within Public Service by the Gauteng Provincial Government. Batho Pele is a South African political initiative that was first introduced by the Mandela Administration in 1997 to stand for the better delivery of goods and services to the public.

Upon further reflection, their success as parents in terms of support and influence has had far more significance on my life and journey than any success that they may see me achieve. For instance, my dad's personal sacrifice to ensure we received the best education possible at the expense of his own material desires – had he not made the investment to place us in a private school, my life would be very different from the path I am on now. This commitment was again demonstrated when making the investment to send me to university, and even after messing around and dropping out after my first year, he still invested in me to go to Technikon to complete my engineering diploma. His selflessness and commitment to the benefit of our family has laid a solid foundation that has created the opportunity for me answer my call to adventure.

I have a totally different perspective and appreciation of my mom's entrepreneurial journey and successes of the preschool, compared to the anger

Chapter 17: The Enablers

I felt many years back. They have groomed and influenced generations of young children who are now active contributing members of society. And at 63, her entrepreneurial flame continues to burn. She is taking all the years of knowledge and experience to create training programmes of excellence for practitioners and administrators in Early Childhood Development. As is the case with Sandisiwe Tsana, who started working at 'Little People' as a domestic worker in June 2007. During 2008, she was given an opportunity to work with the children and had on-the-job training based on the introductory practitioner's course that my mom has designed. In 2009, Sandisiwe won the Forum for Early Childhood Best Practitioner Award.

My relationship with my parents has evolved to one of friendship, and as time passes the dynamic continues to change in the direction of reversing roles, where I am having to parent them in their old age. Failure to launch has not only allowed me to live my dream, but it has also prepared me to one day raise and support a family of my own.

"They tried to bury us. They didn't know we were seeds."
~ Mexican Proverb

PART 3

ATONEMENT

CHAPTER 18
THE STORY BEHIND THE STORY BEHIND THE STORY

Chapter 18
THE STORY BEHIND THE STORY BEHIND THE STORY

While travelling in the USA in 2009, I participated in the Genographic Project at the Detroit Historical Museum. I recall watching a show on National Geographic which spoke about a bold project in partnership with IBM that aimed to help us understand our genetic roots and the migration paths taken by our ancestors. The geek in me couldn't resist, so $100 and a painless cheek swab later, a sample of my DNA was sent to a lab to examine the markers of my Y chromosome. The Y chromosome is passed down from father to son. Ten weeks later and the results for my genetic markers were revealed.

P305 >> M42 >> M168 >> P143 >> M89 >> M578 >> P128 >> M526 >> M214 >> P186

By looking at the above markers, a person can trace their lineage, ancestor by ancestor, to reveal the path they travelled as they moved out of Africa and across the world. P305 tells the story of my earliest ancestor and P186 is my current DNA – of which the location of origin is, surprise surprise – Southeast Asia. Confirmation of my great grandfather Leung Lok Wangon's birthplace.

The common direct paternal ancestor of all men alive today was born in Africa between 300,000 and 150,000 years ago. Around 100,000 years ago the mutation named P305 occurred in the Y chromosome of a man in Africa. Around 80,000 years ago, the BT branch of the Y-chromosome tree was born, defined by many genetic markers, including M42, which saw my ancestors journey out of Africa to the Middle East and India. The man who gave rise to the first genetic marker in my lineage probably lived in northeast Africa in the region of the Rift Valley, perhaps in present-day Ethiopia, Kenya or Tanzania. Scientists put the most likely date for when he lived at around 70,000 years ago. The M168 branch was one of the first to leave the African homeland. The P143 mutation is among the oldest thought

Chapter 18: The Story behind the Story behind the Story

to have occurred outside of Africa and therefore marks a pivotal moment in the evolution of modern humans who first ventured out of the familiar African hunting grounds and into unexplored lands. The first wave of migrants likely ventured across the Bab-al Mandeb strait, a narrow body of water at the southern end of the Red Sea, crossing into the Arabian Peninsula some 60,000 years ago. These beachcombers made their way rapidly to India and Southeast Asia, following the coastline in a gradual march eastward.

The next male ancestor in my ancestral lineage is a man who gave rise to the M89 marker around 55,000 years ago in Middle East. While many of the descendants of M89 remained in the Middle East, others continued to follow the great herds of wild game through what is now modern-day Iran, then north to the Caucasus and the steppes of Central Asia. After settling in Southwest Asia for several millennia, humans began to expand in various directions, including east and south around the Indian Ocean, but also north toward Anatolia and the Black and Caspian Seas.

The first man to acquire mutation M578 some 50,000 years ago was among those who stayed in Southwest Asia before moving on. Fast-forwarding to about 40,000 years ago, the climate shifted once again and became colder and more arid. Drought hit Africa and the Middle East and the grasslands reverted to desert, and for the next 20,000 years, the Saharan Gateway was effectively closed. With the desert impassable, my ancestors had two options: remain in the Middle East, or move on. Retreat to the home continent was not an option.

The next male ancestor in my lineage is the man who gave rise to P128 some 45,000 years ago in South Asia, in what was part of a second wave of migrants who moved east from Southwest Asia. The man who first carried mutation M526 was part of the settlers who migrated around the Indian Ocean and settled in Southeast Asia around 42,000 years ago. Interestingly, this mutation is shared by men from haplogroups M, N, O, P, Q, R and S; these are groups common in East Asia, Southeast Asia, Oceania and the Americas. The M214 branch of my lineage marks another major turning point in my ancestor's journey. The founder of this lineage was a nomad in the time of the Palaeolithic era some 35,000 years ago, eventually leading to my current DNA marker, P186. These ancestors travelled along the coastline of Asia to settle in Southeast Asia for the next 30,000 years. It took my paternal ancestors 100,000 years to migrate from our birthplace in Africa, passing through the Middle East, Iran, India and Asia to eventually settle in Southeast Asia for 30,000 years, before my great grandfather Leung Lok Wangon journeyed from Canton, China in a boat to arrive back on the shores on our birthplace in only two years.

"I am not African because I was born in Africa but because Africa was born in me."
- Kwame Nkrumah

CHAPTER 19
CELEBRATING LIFE AND DIVERSITY

Chapter 19
CELEBRATING LIFE AND DIVERSITY

While the detailed stories of my ancestors through the ages are lost to time, the results from the Genographic Project have brought new meaning to my life. The malicious acts and classifications of an apartheid government that defined us as sub-human no longer have power over me. No longer am I limited or handicapped by the pseudo-science brainwashing that told me who I am, my place in society and what I am capable of. No longer am I scared of the unknown and unfamiliar. How could I be? My ancestors were among those who were courageous enough to leave Africa and venture into the unknown and unfamiliar. They are the survivors and pioneers who have contributed to our human journey over many a millennia.

It gives new meaning to what it means to be 'coloured'. My mixed heritage is a celebration of diversity and love. It represents the true nature of the human spirit and love that is free from prejudice, fear and ignorance.

> *"I am not what happened to me, I am what I chose to become."*
> *~ Carl Jung*

It brings better understanding and clarity which amplifies my relationship with God. I daydream about my ancestors and their journeys through the millennia, thinking about the myths, belief systems and religions that they followed and how these changed over time as their migration from Africa to Southeast Asia unfolded and civilisation evolved, spanning ancient tribal customs and practices to the modern organised religions of Hinduism, Buddhism, Christianity, Judaism, Islam as well as the two Chinese belief systems of Confucianism and Taoism. The sceptic in me still questions the influence, rules, regulations and rituals of colonialism and how Europeans intentionally set out to destroy and greatly modify aspects of traditional cultures with their particular biases and agendas, but I have found peace in celebrating my diverse heritage to shift from apprehension to embracing all myths and all religions in an attempt to identify shared themes, characteristics and values. My devotion to God goes beyond selfish prayers and praise to solicit favour for personal gain, to instead practice surrendering to my own ignorance and the unseen to trust the process and timing of my life.

It has made all the difference in my personal, professional and spiritual life, which is reflected by the many authentic relationships in my life that transcend race, religion, age, gender, class, nationality and sexuality.

> *"Make your God transparent to the transcendent,*
> *and it doesn't matter what his name is."*
> *~ Joseph Campbell, Pathways to Bliss*

CHAPTER 20
DIFFERENT PERSPECTIVES

Chapter 20
DIFFERENT PERSPECTIVES

"We suffer from the delusion that the entire universe is held in order by the categories of human thought."
~ Alan Watts

My personal realization for learning to embrace different perspectives is that I have been guilty on so many occasions of judging people and claiming absolute truths, the source of my personal suffering.

I love gazing at the stars! Have you ever looked up at the night sky and marvelled at the beauty of the stars? You may appreciate their beauty, you may notice patterns or it may inspire you to tell stories. Throughout the ages they have held significance. Our cavemen ancestors stared at them in wonder, giving birth to gods and the heavens, as well as the oldest science of astronomy. Different cultures developed their own interpretation of the stars. The Greeks saw patterns and named constellations after their mythological heroes and legends – Orion was the great hunter. The Egyptians saw patterns too and named constellations after their mythological heroes and legends – Osiris was one of the most important gods of ancient Egypt. The stars were not just for myth, but were used for practical purposes too – navigation and agriculture, before the days of GPS and calendars to navigate the seas and know when to sow crops. Today, we are using the stars to look back into time. Satellite technology like the Hubble Space Telescope is taking pictures of galaxies 100 million light years away – we are seeing the galaxies as they looked 100 million years ago. Scientists have calculated that the observable universe is about 13.8 billion years old, so any light we see in the night sky has been travelling for 13.8 billion years or less to reach us. Calculations indicate that the distance to the edge of the observable universe is about 46 billion light years because the universe is expanding all the time.

Chapter 20: Different Perspectives

The Kepler Space Telescope has also opened a whole new way of looking at stars. Twenty years ago, we didn't know if there were any other planets around any other stars besides our own. We now know that we live in a galaxy that contains more planets than stars. According to astronomers, there are probably more than 170 billion galaxies in the observable universe.

Sunsets are my favourite and I've been privileged enough to have witnessed some of the most beautiful sunsets from the cliffs of Santorini in Greece, the top of Table Mountain in Cape Town, and Fisherman's Wharf overlooking the Golden Gate Bridge in San Francisco. It came as a real surprise to learn that the setting sun is one big optical illusion. As the sun approaches the horizon, the light from it is bent by the different density layers in the atmosphere. The layers curve the light upwards, so the bright glowing orb that you see isn't where you see it. It's below the horizon where you can't 'see' it. It also takes sunlight an average of 8 minutes and 20 seconds to travel from the sun to the earth, so what we are seeing 'already' happened 8 minutes and 20 seconds ago.

My love for travel has seen me visit over 100 major cities across 18 countries on 5 of the 7 continents. Whenever I'd visit a country for the first time, I'd mark it off on a map to keep track of where I've been and where I still want to go. It came as a real surprise to learn about the distortion that occurs when trying to represent our spherical world on a flat piece of paper. Cartographers use a technique called the Mercator projection to morph the globe into a 2D map. One of the most common criticisms of the Mercator map is that it exaggerates the size of countries nearer the poles (US, Russia, Europe), while downplaying the size of those near the equator (the African Continent). To understand the extent of this exaggeration, Greenland appears to be roughly the same size as Africa, when in reality, Greenland is 0.8 million sq. miles and Africa is 11.6 million sq. miles, which is nearly 14.5 times larger.

As a kid, I was always fascinated by rainbows, mainly because of the myth that there was a pot of gold at the end of it. It came as a real surprise to learn that the existence of a rainbow depends on the conical photoreceptors in our eyes. To animals without cones, the rainbow does not exist.

Dogs only have two cones, for blue and yellow – so their rainbow looks quite a bit duller than ours.

Butterflies may have up to five cone receptors and can see many more colours than we can.

The late Japanese author, researcher and entrepreneur Masaru Emoto claimed that human consciousness influences the molecular structure of water and that emotional 'energies' and vibrations' could change the physical structure of the liquid. Emoto's water crystal experiments consisted of exposing water to different words, pictures or music, and then freezing and examining the aesthetic properties of the resulting crystals with microscopic photography. Exposing the water to positive intentions through prayer, speech and thoughts would result in visually pleasing crystals being formed when that water was frozen, and that negative intentions would yield 'ugly' frozen crystal formations. While the research has been criticised by the scientific community for lack of experimental controls, it is worth considering that the human body is made up of 60% water.

As a kid growing up in a broken society, I was ever conscious of the traits that made us and others inferior or superior to ultimately spread and perpetuate hate. If racial slurs didn't get under your skin, then the focus shifted to your sexual orientation. Being gay was condemned and considered sinful. It came as a real surprise to me when reading The Kybalion and learning about the hermetic philosophies of ancient Egypt and Greece and how they interpreted gender. The Principle of Gender focuses on masculine and feminine energies which manifest in both males and females. These masculine and feminine energies are subject to the laws of attraction – positive and negative poles. Does this ancient philosophy then support LGBTQ and pansexual movements to nullify the concept of homosexuality as a man-made construct which follows traditional biases and prejudices? And what of other man-made concepts like money, religion, national boundaries, land ownership and terrorism etc. etc. – we really are the architects of our own suffering!

In Why quantum physicists never fail, author Greg Kuhn shares the story of the late Dr Candice Pert, an internationally recognised neuroscientist and pharmacologist who published over 250 research articles and pioneered the emergence of Mind-Body Medicine, where she discovered that thoughts are real, physical things. Every thought you have has a unique neuropeptide associated with it, and your body in turn produces that unique neuropeptide every time you experience that particular thought (and its associated emotion). A neuropeptide is a simple, protein-based amino acid that is produced by your hypothalamus, the 'control centre' at the base of your brain. Your thoughts 'translate' into unique neuropeptides and literally become molecular messengers of emotion. Neuropeptides flood your bloodstream in the billions and are physically assimilated by your body's cells, inserting themselves into a special receptacle on the cell membrane, just like a key fitting into a keyhole. Over time, cells develop more and more unique receptacles on their membranes to capture the neuropeptides to which they are most often exposed. The process can be compared to a person with an addiction to a chemical substance. It stresses the importance and impact of our thoughts as well as our body's native repair and regenerative systems for natural healing.

Letting go of my prejudices and indifference requires constant work and awareness. My only saving grace is that my journey keeps me honest – instead of judging and claiming absolute truths, I now consider the reasons why I am being indifferent and threatened by somebody else's truth and the way they perceive the world, rather than by who they are or what they are saying or doing. I also question my indifference as a result of my own fears and insecurities, letting go of the illusions of safety and security that have been imposed on me, or even worse, the ones that I impose on myself.

CHAPTER 21

FINDING PURPOSE THROUGH ENTREPRENEURSHIP

Chapter 21
FINDING PURPOSE THROUGH ENTREPRENEURSHIP

*"An equation means nothing to me unless it
expresses a thought of God."*
~ Srinivasa Ramanujan

Entrepreneurship can't be taught; it is lived. For me, it's a lifestyle, a means to express my creativity. My journey into entrepreneurship is anything but planned or intended. It is the culmination of a lifetime of events and context that have been influenced by my curiosity, rebelliousness, stubbornness, ambition and relentless persistence, with twists of love and deep pain. It has brought with it many challenges that I've had to overcome, the biggest of which was getting over myself – letting go of old limiting beliefs and habits, unlearning what I was taught at home, in school, university and corporate, while learning new beliefs and skills of abundance that have empowered me to navigate the unknown and deal with the constant uncertainty, the unfamiliar, failure, rejection and setbacks. And despite all my failures and losses to date, I am more excited than ever about the possibilities and opportunities that are, and will be available in our lifetime, as well as my potential to play a part in it.

In his book, Zero to One: Notes on Start-ups, or How to Build the Future, legendary entrepreneur and investor Peter Thiel asks a contrarian question: "What important truth do very few people agree with you on?" It becomes even more difficult to answer when the question is followed up with: "So what do you intend to do about it?", noting that "Brilliant thinking is rare, but courage is in even shorter supply than genius".

*"People don't need to be saved or rescued. People need knowledge
of their own power, and how to access it."*
~ Tammy Plunkett

Chapter 21: Finding Purpose through Entrepreneurship

What important truth do very few people agree with me on? I believe that there is greatness within all of us to achieve our individual and grandest aspirations, and that success does not have to be at the expense of others. It is a truth that few people agree with me on and this is evident in the amount of current inequality and disparities across all aspects of our lives, where success takes the shape of a pyramid – most people are stuck at the base slaving away so that a very few can get to enjoy the view from the top.

I believe that this current reality is a product of our thinking, which is based on Newtonian paradigms, more than any intentional evil at play. One of the by-products of Newtonian paradigms is scarcity, and this scarcity mindset is a fundamental thread in the fabric of our current thought process.

So, what do I intend to do about it? One of Albert Einstein's quotes had puzzled me for years: ***"We cannot solve our problems with the same thinking we used when we created them"***. It was only once I started to understand and apply the paradigms of quantum physics and other thought experiments that I understood what Einstein meant by our "thinking". One of the by-products of quantum physics paradigms is abundance, and this abundance mindset is a game changer in creating a new narrative for a society that is inclusive for everybody to participate in.

It is interesting to observe the growth that a person goes through when answering their call to adventure into the unknown and unfamiliar. In my personal journey, I've grown from an emotional wreck, allowing my emotions to define who I was, to a person of extreme calm – I handle my biggest failures and greatest successes in the same stride. My emotions don't control me anymore like they use to – they are a compass to alert me if my beliefs and desires are aligned. Intellectually, I started out wanting to solve the world's problems, relentless in my pursuit for answers. Now, the answers don't matter as much as the questions I ask. I no longer want to change the world or solve its problems, rather I occupy my time trying to discover alternate narratives that are more inclusive and equitable. Physically, I am fitter and stronger than I have ever been in my life, so I am able to endure and give more of myself, and while I don't quite know how it works, my body's native repair and regenerative systems for self-healing ensures I stay healthy and am no longer easily prone to illness. Spiritually, I've grown from a place of darkness to find peace and purpose, where my relationship with God is free from thought. I share the sentiment of the strange but brilliant Indian mathematician Srinivasa Ramanujan and would modify his quote to read, "An **idea** means nothing to me unless it expresses a thought of God".

I certainly have come a long way since reflecting on "who I was, who I had become, and who I wanted to be", all those years back. My destination is my journey and my hunger to grow is still the same even as I reflect today, evident in my openness to learn more about myself and the universe and my willingness to change – which is still an unpleasant process. If the most painful life lesson I've learnt is that we are the contextual creators of our life experiences, then the hardest lesson in life is learning to unlearn the things that give rise to, or which manifest our contextual realities for life experiences that serve us, instead of those that cause us suffering.

In Zero to One, 'Zero' represents horizontal progress where we see intensive or incremental improvements on things we already know, whereas 'One' represents vertical progress where we see extensive or exponential improvements – this progress is harder to imagine because it requires doing something that nobody else has ever done – and this is the space I prefer to play in – the things we don't know we don't know. 'Zero' could represent the Newtonian paradigms of mechanism, determinism, separateness or logical outcomes, and 'One' could represent the quantum physics paradigms of holism, unity, entanglement or nonlinearity. It is not about which thinking style is better, but more about incorporating more ways of thinking about business and life to produce more options that are more equitable and inclusive with significantly better results.

Take crime for example. A 'separateness' paradigm means we see ourselves and the criminal as two distinct and separate observers of a crime being committed. The 'determinism' paradigm says that for every action, there is an equal and opposite reaction, so the criminal is the aggressor and therefore must be punished. The 'logical outcomes' paradigm says we need more police to catch criminals, more jails and prisons to make sure our communities are safe. This reality is a process of our thinking.

Chapter 21: Finding Purpose through Entrepreneurship

From a quantum physics paradigm perspective, the 'entanglement' paradigm says we are all connected and not detached observers without influence in the experience that is unfolding; we just have different perspectives of the same experience. The 'unity' paradigm says that actions are not the most important component of any event and that our physical reality is exactly what we expect to see and experience – mainstream media and the general negativity in our social interactions ensure we are reminded daily about crime and the violent nature thereof. The 'nonlinearity' paradigm says there is no logical sequence, correlation or cohesion to events and that systems are not proportional to their causes – people turn to crime, but not for the reasons we may think. An alternative reality based on quantum physics paradigms means we would see crime as a symptom rather than a cause and be open to more possibilities in solving it. I would never justify any crime and I am aware of the devastating impact it can have on the victims and their families, but I also don't believe that anybody is born with aspirations to one day become a criminal or cause harm to others. I don't claim to know the answers either, but I have made a commitment to dedicate my life to trying to make a difference in creating more opportunities for people to be successful. Employing more police and building more jails may improve crime statistics, but consider that providing better access to quality education and employment opportunities for all could significantly reduce and even eradicate crime. Education and an inclusive collaborative economy are just two of many nonlinear initiatives in solving crime. This scenario extends beyond just thinking differently, as it also speaks to our behaviour and actions. If we didn't see ourselves as 'separate' observers to a crime, but as 'connected' and equal participants in crime, which is the result of an inherently flawed system, would we become more active as citizens in how we engage each other, and in our relationship with and expectations of government, and vice versa? On a lighter note, my favourite analogy of this evolution in thinking and business is photography. Growing up the 80s and 90s, I was a keen photographer, but it was an intensive and expensive process. The cameras were bulky and used spools that needed to be developed. Only once developed would you be able to separate the good pictures from the bloopers, and once in an album, people would have to take turns to view the pictures. I recall the hours spent scrapbooking to create albums that are now stored in a filing cabinet collecting dust. Then came digital cameras which were great, as photos could be viewed and edited on a PC before being printed, and Photoshop meant scrapbooking was now digital. Even so, people would still have to gather around the PC and take turns to view the pictures. Then came the internet, and then the smartphone which replaced the need for a digital camera, and probably the most significant developments to redefine and disrupt photography have been Facebook and Apps. We probably all take it for granted the ability to take a picture, add a filter or make a collage and then instantly share it with anybody in our social networks, not to mention the new types of engagements made possible through social networks.

This type of disruption is occurring across all industries to the point of a distinct pattern and an almost guaranteed certainty. Peter Diamantis best describes it in his book 'Bold: How to Go Big, Create Wealth, and Impact the World' as the 6 Ds Framework: Digitised, Deceptive, Disruptive, Dematerialised, Demonetised, Democratised. And in an age of information, the underlying exponential technologies driving this pattern to democratisation include infinite computing, sensors, artificial intelligence, networks, robotics, digital manufacturing, synthetic biology, digital medicine, virtual and augmented reality, nanomaterials and 3D printing. Business models and access to these technologies are changing too. Before, they were only available to large corporations and governments, yet today you can access these technologies as an individual with just a laptop and an internet connection. When you consider that 3,1 billion people had internet access in 2015 and that this will rise to over 5 billion people by 2020 – the opportunities and applications thereof are only limited by our imagination and persistence.

More than democratisation, it is the infinite possibilities for creating value in people's lives that is becoming a reality that can no longer be ignored. Avoidance comes at the expense of becoming irrelevant and ultimately bankrupt. The famous use cases are Kodak and Blockbuster, but this will be extended to an individual level with many jobs becoming obsolete in the near future. If that's hard to imagine, just reflect on the 'Deceptive' phase of the 6 D's framework.

Chapter 21: Finding Purpose through Entrepreneurship

Depending on your current narrative, it could mark a stage of doom and gloom, or it could just be the greatest time in our history as a species to be alive – a period of abundant opportunity that is inclusive and accessible to all who dare dream! It is only a matter of time before conversations shift from what is your job, to how do you occupy your time?

For me personally, it has brought purpose to my life, and that purpose can be summed up in three words:

Unleash Human Potential

www.ingramcontent.com/pod-product-compliance
Lightning Source LLC
Chambersburg PA
CBHW061321040426
42444CB00011B/2720